SLAM

Build your startup idea
or early stage business
with the Startup Launch
Assistance Map

JON WARNER

SLAM. Build your startup idea or early stage business with the Startup Launch Assistance Map.
Published by: Team Publications Pty Ltd
First edition: July 2019
Author: Jon Warner
Cover and internal design by Kerry Milin, Production Works
Printed in the United States of America

ISBN: 978-1-51-3651-06-4

Disclaimer

Who will benefit from reading this book?

Every author likes to believe that a wide variety of people from all over the world will read his or her book. However, with business books like this in particular, the truth is that it is often a very specific niche that really benefits from the experience. The broad group of readers who are most targeted by this book are obviously anyone interested in startups and entrepreneurship as a subject. However, this breaks down into three areas as follows:

Individuals who constantly have ideas or think about new or different ways to do things in life but have never acted on it formally. This book helps by suggesting a path to validate that his or her thinking/idea is on-point and capable of potentially becoming a commercial venture of some kind. For example, this may be a college student or professor looking to evolve a project and license it, or any person who thinks an idea might become a small or even large business one day.

Individuals who are working in a larger company who have one or more 'side-hustles' and believe that one of these has the potential to employ them (and others) perhaps full-time in the future. This book assists by not only helping to validate that the side-hustle can grow and support them but also to outline the execution path that is necessary. For example, this may be a person who sells a product or service online on a website like 'Shopify' mainly in the evenings or weekends and thinks this may have more potential to grow.

Individuals who run or already work in a startup or early-stage company (or in some cases run a new division of a larger company) and want to ensure that their efforts to date haven't missed any important steps (which he or she can revisit) or even help turbo-charge what is already being done and both de-risk their efforts and perhaps make the business more investable to outsiders. This book helps by offering two 8-step templates, which provide questions in response to which good answers should exist, or be found. For example, this may be a startup founder who has spent many months and a lot of 'boot-strapped' cash to establish a small business but now needs to convince outsiders of its future value and success potential.

Whichever category best fits, and some people reading this book will not fit into any of these categories, I hope the path described is an interesting one.

About the author

Five-time company CEO, Jon Warner is a widely respected entrepreneurship expert having founded and led three startups (with one failure, one that did not 'trouble the scorer' and one successful exit). Jon's career started in the corporate world with Air Products, working in the US and across Europe before joining Exxon-Mobil. At Exxon-Mobil Jon worked in the UK, the US, Australia, and Nigeria, ending his career there as Deputy CEO.

Following his 15 years in the corporate world, Jon founded and grew a management consulting business called The Worldwide Center for Organizational Development which had over 20 people carrying out a range of strategy assignments for large national and global companies. Much of this work focused on building an innovative culture and establishing greater internal entrepreneurship skills.

Jon was also CEO of two other startups – a digital publishing company and a bill-pay and payments software platform that operated in the US, UK, and Australia. Since his exit from the latter, Jon has been working from a California base to mentor and invest in disruptive startup companies, especially in the area of technology deployment and healthcare and aging technology in particular. Jon is CEO of Silver Moonshots, a research organization and 'virtual incubator' for startups focused on the 50+ population.

Jon is a noted speaker at businesses, colleges and conferences across the world. He also lectures on entrepreneurship at both undergraduate and MBA level at UCLA, UCR Riverside and at the University of Redlands, all in Southern California, where he is based.

Jon is also a prolific author having published 40 books, all concerning business, management, leadership, entrepreneurship and innovation.

Jon is a graduate of the UK top-five Warwick University, with a double bachelor's degree in philosophy and politics and an MBA (with a finance specialism). JON also has a PhD in psychology specializing in neuro-science.

Contents

Foreword

I took my first engineering design course as an undergraduate in 1975. One of our assignments was to design a way for people in wheelchairs to access books that were out of reach on library bookshelves. As part of the design process, we tromped off to the college library and imagined ourselves sitting in a wheelchair in the stacks. We then went to our drawing boards (this was before AutoCAD) and drew up variations on the theme of a reach extender with a hand-grip that would allow someone to pull a book off the shelf and lower it into his or her lap. The one thing none of us did (that I know of) was to actually talk to a person in a wheelchair to see what his or her unmet need was. If we had, we might have discovered that they were unable to even read a book or hold one successfully and turn the pages. In fact, we might have discovered that what they really wanted was something that looked more like a Kindle or an iPad with an electronic voice reader that would not require going to the library at all. We were warned by our instructor, not to be 'functionally fixed,' and yet we were completely stuck by the notion that books had to be acquired in a library. The absence of user feedback doomed our designs to irrelevance, although we were all very proud of them.

For my junior project, my engineering class was challenged to design a power pack that could be attached to a conventional wheelchair and make it self-propelled. We devised a system with a steering motor, a drive motor that powered a fifth wheel, and a battery that hooked on the back of the wheelchair. Once again we did not talk to any potential users. Our design worked fine on a flat surface but was underpowered to go up a ramp. Without user input, we had lots of fun but we had no idea if we were actually meeting an unmet need.

In my remaining engineering courses in mechanical and aeronautical engineering, we did a lot of analysis but very little actual design work, except for small subsystems. The assumption was that customer needs were something someone else would determine and we would design to follow suit.

In the 1980s I studied marketing and strategy as part of my MBA program. Our marketing instructor had a memorable matrix he called 'wants and gots' that he used to organize his market research. Wants were what Jon Warner would call unmet needs. Gots were what the SLAM model would call the product or service offering. While the list was helpful at identifying ways in which an existing product might be succeeding at meeting customer needs, we never discussed how to change the product to fill the gap. I remember asking him what defined a successful marketing strategy and his reply was 'go where the customers are.' At the time, I took that to be a geographic argument for locating your business wisely. An entire industry in spatial analysis has arisen to meet that need, but geography was only part of the answer. The real meaning of 'go where your customers are' is to meet the unmet need. When you do, you don't have to sell the product or service. People will rush to get it. I was close to understanding this process, but somehow I had still missed it.

After getting my Ph.D., I did a lot of work designing a curriculum for my business school. Sometimes the programs I designed were moderately successful and sometimes they barely moved the needle. They were designed based on the needs of my faculty to teach interesting subjects and a vague sense of what was needed in the business community.

As a hobby, I updated components of a vintage airplane I was restoring. These projects included new wing spars and new brakes as well as an updated instrument panel and modern electrical system with starter, alternator, and appropriate modern radios. These projects were designed to please me not a larger customer base.

I started attending design-thinking workshops at conferences and used what I learned in several of my courses. In all of the 'quick and dirty' design exercises I participated in, we'd spend about five minutes interviewing potential users for our designs, then went right into the 'minimum viable prototype' phase of the process. The resulting designs were fun to see and enjoyable to create, but it is doubtful that they really met an unmet need. For one thing, we were usually redesigning an existing project or service such as a shopping basket or a course syllabus, not beginning from the need and thinking deeply about what product or service could best meet that need.

In 2015, I was visiting old friends in Canada doing research for a book project about our work together in Bangladesh in the 1980s. One of my friends had gone into the water purification business because he hated the fact that we had to boil off our drinking water to stay safe because the local groundwater was contaminated. He mentioned one of his clients had invented as space age shower that cleaned water as it was used, lowering both energy costs and water use by up to 90 percent. I started thinking about how nice it would be to have a shower after a hot hike and wondered whether it could be made portable. I now had an idea for a business.

To pursue the idea I split my business class up into several groups, each researching a different potential use for the portable shower. They looked at fire camps, temporary homeless shelters, campgrounds, beach parks, and outdoor events such as music festivals and cross-country motorcycle races. Working collaboratively with students at a French university, they came back with various estimates of feasibility and created a simple design schematic for the shower.

That spring, I obtained a used trailer from a friend and with a student gathered up components, raising money from a GoFundMe campaign. By the end of the summer in 2017, we had the shower running. Three more students came forward to work on the project in fall 2017 and spring 2018 and we all presented the business at a Startup Pitch Competition. While the project did not win, it did get a lot of positive feedback from the judges and it introduced me to Jon Warner.

Jon and I started meeting on a regular basis and he quickly asked how many customers had we actually talked to? The answer was none. We put together the prototype on the basis of my ideas about what would work or what wouldn't. I was OK with something simple and rough to test the concept. It never occurred to me that the shower itself might not be the ideal product to meet an unmet need big enough to justify bringing it to market.

Over the fall of 2018 and the spring of 2019, groups of students contacted potential users for the shower, searching for the unmet need without disclosing what our product actually was. The going was very slow at first but eventually, we started to learn from real people we met that handled disasters at water companies, hospitals, and government agencies whose job it was to put resources in place before a disaster strikes. As we asked about their needs, we learned how expensive it is to transport bottled water, and how expensive current filtration systems can be. We also learned that melted plastic puts benzene into the public water supply after a wildfire and that animal waste is a big contaminator after flooding in rural areas. We learned that the need for our product was not sufficient immediately after a disaster and that it was in the months between the first response and the restoration of the water, power, transportation, and telecom grid.

A shower on a trailer could not be transported over a closed road or brought in by helicopter or small boat. It would be too big. The modular units could be sold to individuals as part of their personal disaster preparedness or to institutions such as local governments around a region because events such as earthquakes can affect a large area and the specific location is impossible to predict. One person we spoke to summed it up. He had gone to Puerto Rico after the hurricane. His response was simple: If we had a portable water unit available for those missions, he would have taken everything we could supply. That is the sign that the SLAM process is working when the potential customer hears the idea and says, 'When can I get it?'

The feedback totally changed our thinking as a result of using the SLAM process. We know the solution must be very portable, no bigger than a large toolbox. It could be modular, with separate units for purification, heating, and power generation. The water might be used for drinking, but it should also be available for washing clothes, dishes, and bodies. We learned that our service has an acronym: WASH for Water, Sanitation, and Hygiene.

Because of the SLAM process, we are now applying for an innovation grant from the National Institute of Health. My prototype shower served its purpose. We can take it apart and reassemble the components into a smaller set of units, or design the new modules from scratch. Even better, we can continue our customer discovery and market research knowing we are on a productive path that will result in an economically viable product that meets an unmet need for a large population. We can't wait to go on to the next phase of the project. The SLAM process got us ready to move forward with confidence.

As you can see, I know from personal experience that Jon Warner's SLAM process fills a strong need in the literature of innovation and entrepreneurship. Its singular contribution is the emphasis on the match between the unmet need in the market and the product or service offered by the entrepreneur. This core requirement for success is underplayed or overlooked in the engineering, design thinking, innovation, and entrepreneurship literature but this small book fills that gap.

James Spee, PhD, Professor
University of Redlands, School of Business, California,
June 2019

Preface

This book started as an 8-page article written in early 2018 on a new process that I had developed called the Startup Launch Assistance Map or SLAM. This process came about as a result of working with a wide variety of entrepreneurs and startup founders during the year before the article was written. This allowed me time to hone the system and test that all the prompting advice it offered was easily understood and useful to individuals in practical ways. This book takes that 8-page article much further in three main ways:

- Firstly, it clearly expands greatly on the concepts and gives the reader a much deeper explanation of what every step involves thinking about or carefully considering.

- Secondly, this book includes a detailed case study to show how one business (a group of food trucks) could apply the SLAM process at each progressive step.

- Thirdly, the book describes a complimentary but additional process with the Goal, Results, Action Navigational Device or GRAND. This process, which emerged from the need for a better startup execution or implementation system, once their ideas were deemed feasible, follows the same 8-step process and has the case study to apply each of these.

My hope is that the GRAND SLAM processes are useful to any entrepreneur, if only as a checklist to consider along the way.

Launching a startup, or for that matter any newly established small business in any sector is often an extremely difficult path to take and we need all the tools we can to reduce the risks of the journey ahead as well as provide as much useful impetus as possible.

Introduction

In 2010, Alexander Osterwalder and Yves Pigneur wrote the book *Business Model Generation: A Handbook For Visionaries, Game Changers, and Challengers.*

This book was written to be highly consistent with much of the thinking promulgated by the 'lean startup' initiative, inspired, among others, by entrepreneurship professor Steve Blank (then at Stanford University in California) and built upon and promoted widely by Eric Reiss and many others.

Since this time, the book's great innovation was, and has continued to be, to create a 'business model canvas' with nine boxes on one page for startup founders to fill out in draft and then test and re-test their ideas in real-world interviews with potential customers and make the necessary adjustments. In other words, this approach almost completely retired the old idea that a 30- to 40-page business plan was a prerequisite to starting a business and a necessary condition before money could be raised (although some banks and others still insist on this even today!).

Osterwalder and Pigneur's book, and the single page canvas completion approach they recommend (shown in the chart overleaf), was nothing short of transformational and in the last few years its use has become commonplace in startup incubators, accelerators, educational institutions, and entrepreneurial consulting practices of all sizes, including in government circles all over the world. For example, it is now included in the US National Science Foundation's i-Corp program. It has, therefore, become truly national and international at scale and created a whole new language for entrepreneurs to use. All entrepreneurs, old and new, therefore owe a great deal to all of the people individuals involved in the lean startup movement and this book certainly stands on the shoulders of these giant and revolutionary thinkers.

As effective and widespread as it has been, especially in helping to encourage startups to think about 'product-market fit' (shown as the

Key Partners

What are our key Partners?
Who are our key Suppliers?
Which Key Resources are we acquiring from partners?
Which Key Activities do partners perform?

Key Activities

What Key Activities do our Value Propositions require?
Our Distribution Channels?
Customer Relationships?
Revenue streams?

Key Resources

What Key Resources do our Value Propositions require?
Our Distribution Channels? Customer Relationships?
Revenue Streams?

Value Propositions

What value do we deliver to the customer?
Which one of our customer's problems are we helping to solve?
What bundles of products and services are we offering to each Customer Segment?
Which customer needs are we satisfying?

Customer Relationships

What type of relationship does each of our Customer Segments expect us to establish and maintain with them?
Which ones have we established?
How are they integrated with the rest of our business model?
How costly are they?

Channels

Through which Channels do our Customer Segments want to be reached?
How are we reaching them now?
How are our Channels integrated?
Which ones work best?
Which ones are most cost-efficient?
How are we integrating them with customer routines?

Customer Segments

For whom are we creating value?
Who are our most important customers?

Cost Structure

What are the most important costs inherent in our business model?
Which Key Resources are most expensive?
Which Key Activities are most expensive?

Revenue Streams

For what value are our customers really willing to pay?
For what do they currently pay?
How are they currently paying?
How would they prefer to pay?
How much does each Revenue Stream contribute to overall revenues?

Above: Business model canvas used with permission from Strategyzer

2

relationship between the value proposition in the center of the chart and the particular target customer segment, shown on the far right) the main problem many founders experience with the business model canvas is that the right-hand side of the chart gets used but not so much the left-hand side, at least not rigorously.

In addition, there is no direct sequence recommended for each of these nine panels on the canvas itself, although it is suggested in the supporting text. Moreover, although the canvas does not purport to be all-encompassing, it does omit some important considerations at the earliest stages of a startup, such as identifying a startup's competition and conducting a careful and detailed market sizing exercise.

It is for these reasons and others that the SLAM diagram, which we will describe next, is a somewhat different or alternative approach.

Introduction to the SLAM process

In an attempt to provide a remedy for the issues that many ideators and early-stage startups experience with the business model canvas, we will describe an alternative but complimentary approach that startups can take. We call this the Startup Launch Assistance Map (SLAM).

The SLAM process, illustrated on the next page, is an 8-step sequential process, starting on the left, moving across the center to the right, establishing the key boxes needed to consider product market fit, or as we prefer to call it, 'market-product fit' and then going clockwise thereafter.

As you will see, the SLAM is the first of two processes that we will be describing, with the Goal, Results, Action Navigational Device (GRAND) also being a similar 8-step process that should be considered only once the SLAM diagram (which should be completed slowly and rigorously) is complete.

SLAM is not intended to be a *replacement* for the business model canvas, as the supporting material for this methodology is now deep and extensive. It is suggested to be *complementary* to it, perhaps best used as an earlier step, either as a standalone exercise or to complete before later transferring some of the information into the business model canvas and then adding more information there (although it will also easily suffice on standalone basis). However it is used, we

The Startup Launch Assistance Map (SLAM)

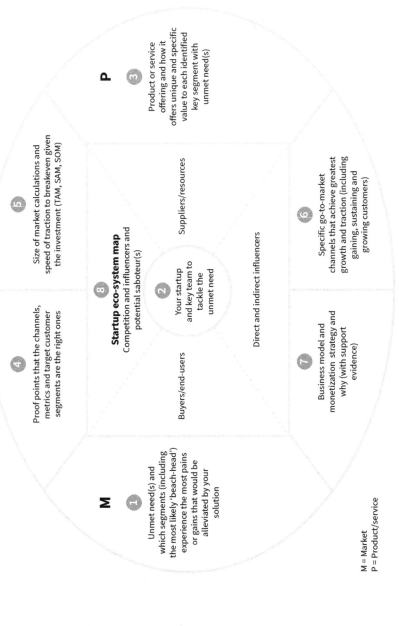

P

3 — Product or service offering and how it offers unique and specific value to each identified key segment with unmet need(s)

5 — Size of market calculations and speed of traction to breakeven given the investment (TAM, SAM, SOM)

Startup eco-system map
Competition and influencers and potential saboteur(s)

Suppliers/resources

2 — Your startup and key team to tackle the unmet need

Direct and indirect influencers

4 — Proof points that the channels, metrics and target customer segments are the right ones

Buyers/end-users

6 — Specific go-to-market channels that achieve greatest growth and traction (including gaining, sustaining and growing customers)

7 — Business model and monetization strategy and why (with support evidence)

M

1 — Unmet need(s) and which segments (including the most likely 'beach-head') experience the most pains or gains that would be alleviated by your solution

M = Market
P = Product/service

have seen the SLAM diagram or map used successfully in a wide variety of new ventures or companies of many types.

This sequential diagram is a simple but powerful way for startup teams, individual ideators and founders, and even mature businesses with new products or services, to help assess their entrepreneurial thinking and hypotheses and judge whether or not they have an idea they can commercially scale.

It should be noted that there is inevitably some entrepreneurial or startup terminology and jargon that is used throughout this book. While some of it is explained as we go, some may need further investigation by searching online to more fully appreciate the depth of the thinking or concept. To make this a little easier on the reader, a glossary of over 100 terms used in the book is included at the end for quick reference.

How to use the SLAM diagram

There are two main ways in which the SLAM diagram can be used:

1. When an individual identifies an issue or challenge for a customer group that may need a new or different solution and has a relatively loose or vague idea about what could be done – we call this *ideation.*
2. When an individual (often with other person(s) recruited to the cause) has decided to jump into a venture, often part-time, to build a solution for an issue that has been identified, for which they think they have a broad solution – we call this *entrepreneurialism.*

Using the SLAM diagram for ideation

In many ways, whether it is for ideation or entrepreneurialism, completing it early on is the ideal time to use the SLAM diagram, because it is a process that helps to frame the issue or problem being addressed (What is it? When does it occur? What form does it take? Do various people experience it differently? Which group of people experience the issue the most and why? etc.).

At this early stage, the SLAM process is testing the *feasibility* of an idea that has the potential to become an entrepreneurial venture and/or testing the wisdom of expending resources on a possible startup and even deciding upon how much money is spent on the effort and in what ways.

In this case, the initial completion of the SLAM process is usually done by one person alone (the ideator) and then customer discovery is conducted by that individual to test all the assumptions and hypotheses (even if it is discussed with others subsequently).

Using the SLAM diagram for entrepreneurialism

While it's highly effective for ideators, even later stage entrepreneurs can gain much from using the SLAM process before they have 'burned' too much of their own or family and friends' time and money, and certainly before they have raised any external funding that will be expected to provide a return in a reasonable time frame. In this case, the SLAM process usefully starts by encouraging a careful thinking phase by listing the 'unmet need(s)' or problem(s) the entrepreneur believes he or she is solving and how, with the team currently on hand or available, a possible solution can be tested or *validated*.

In the above situation, 'validation' means reassessing whether the target need/pain and customers are the right or most appropriate ones, and, once done, whether or not this target group values the proposed product or service that is being suggested.

In most circumstances, customer discovery here tends to lead to minor adjustments or what are often called small or large scale 'pivots' to get closer to market-product fit (which we will describe in more detail later).

It cannot be stressed enough, and as we will say several times in this book, customer discovery is critical to the ideator and entrepreneur. Quite simply, the greater the volume of perceived target customer interviews, the more the potential commercialization of a new idea or concept is 'de-risked'. The SLAM diagram is the ideal place to note this feedback and make continual changes until a coherent and consistent story arises that is executable. This is a very different approach to the most commonly adopted startup strategy – build a basic version of the product or service and see if customers will then buy it. We argue this is a frustrating and often expensive way to do things.

The 8 steps of the SLAM process

As mentioned earlier, the SLAM process has two sides to it (often printed as the front and back of a single page). These are:

- the SLAM process which helps to evaluate the feasibility or longer-term viability of an idea for a possible or actual startup; and

- the GRAND process (which we only get to when we have completed the SLAM side) which helps to plan the execution steps to heighten the possibility that a startup gains traction and thrives in the medium- to long-term.

Both sides have eight steps on them and we will start with the eight steps of the SLAM process. But before doing this, why are there eight steps and what might be missing?

There are literally thousands of books that will not only describe companies that were once startups, and what they did to plan and gain traction or scale over time, and also offer helpful advice on what investors often look for in a startup or early-stage company pitch. In addition, there are many books, booklets, articles and websites offering checklists for startup founders to use to think about a range of issues that need to be carefully considered.

What the SLAM process does is two main things with eight steps including:

1. Synthesizing much of the above advice into the eight most commonly mentioned and deemed to be important steps to consider, especially at the earliest stages of the startup's life.

2. Sequencing these steps to allow the information to be built progressively and iteratively in a simple fashion (as some information in later steps may change or adjust the thoughts and ideas listed at earlier steps).

Let's now describe each of the eight steps in a little more detail in two ways:

- By describing the step in general and then by summarizing what needs to be considered in the three key questions you can and should be asking.

- By offering a case study on a fictitious food truck business called Fresh-Fare. This is a simple Business to Customer (B2C) business to help show how these ideas can be put into practice.

To provide a little base information and color on this food truck business, a few background notes are provided on the next page.

Food truck case study

Background

A food truck is a kitchen/restaurant on wheels. Compared to a fixed 'brick and mortar' restaurant, it saves money on rent, equipment, food preparation time, and by having simpler menu items, but has similar costs in terms of labor and ingredient supplies (depending on the type of food truck focus).

In the case study that is described throughout this book (with the truck icon used to distinguish these pages) the Fresh-Fare food truck business is a dream for Laguna Hills, California residents, a husband and wife team, Hector and Maria. Both are in their early 50s, with two children, aged 18 and 19.

Hector retired early when offered an attractive package by his long-term employer. Hector worked in his father's restaurant as a teen for several years and enjoyed it. Maria is currently a senior accounting assistant but did several years of waitressing in her 20s while attending college.

They have around $150,000 of their own capital in the bank to spend on their dream project.

Having done some research into the food truck industry, Hector and Maria know that they can buy their first truck new for $200,000 and second-hand for $50,000 but they want to make the first one a success before building this up to what they hope will be six trucks over a period of five years, operating all over Southern California.

They want to offer a 'green' eating experience, which means sustainable processes and as much organic and healthy food as possible.

A good rule of thumb is that an average food truck charges $10 per cover and needs 150 covers a day to make a 10% net return. If one truck does this, it will make around $375,000 a year, presuming that it can operate 250 days a year.

Note: Although we are describing a food truck business, all of the descriptions of the issues and decisions taken should have direct crossover applicability to any startup. Readers might therefore want to think carefully about the parallels with what they have in mind for their own startup as the case study unfolds.

Ten US food truck industry background facts

1. The food truck Industry in the US has revenues of over $1 billion in 2019.

2. There are almost 24,000 food trucks in the US as of 2019, most of these in urban areas. Some of these are small vans and some are large RV-type vehicles.

3. Labor costs are typically 20% to 25% of food truck revenues and food purchases typically account for 40% of revenues.

4. The food trucks industry has experienced a boom over the five years to 2019, primarily as a result of the surge in gastronomy in the United States. The industry is composed of operators that prepare and serve a broad range of cuisine from mobile food trucks on city sidewalks, in parks and at events. Over the past five years, the industry has outpaced the broader food-service sector. Additionally, the industry has evolved quickly, as entrepreneurial food truck operators have entered the market to cater to changing consumer preferences in favor of gourmet offerings and unique food concepts.

5. Food trucks offer convenient and affordable meals and snacks in areas with high foot traffic including work sites, busy shopping centers and intersections, sporting events, college campuses and cultural events. Consequently, demand for food trucks largely depends on location, with the most successful food trucks being located in busy areas.

6. As food trucks compete with quick-service restaurants and a variety of other food-service providers, operators must offer unique menu items to drive demand.

7. Laws governing food trucks differ by city, with most specifying the hours during which food trucks can operate and the distance they must be from the nearest brick-and-mortar restaurant.

8. Most food trucks operate in urban locations where population density is high and per capita disposable income is higher than average. As the urban population increases, the industry's pool of potential customers grows.

9. The barriers to entry into the food trucks industry are low when compared with other food-service sector businesses.

10. Consumers are becoming more aware of health issues associated with fatty food intake and are increasingly going out of their way to avoid such foods. Traditionally, food trucks specialized in lower-end, fried foods. Conversely, an increase in healthy attitudes toward food can benefit food trucks that sell healthy products.

Products and services segmentation (2019)

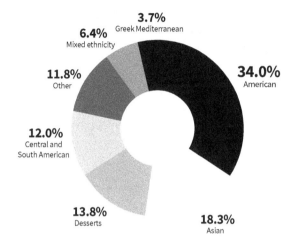

3.7% Greek Mediterranean

6.4% Mixed ethnicity

11.8% Other

34.0% American

12.0% Central and South American

13.8% Desserts

18.3% Asian

Major market segmentation (2019)

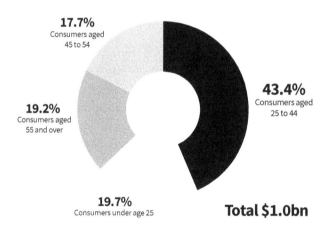

17.7% Consumers aged 45 to 54

19.2% Consumers aged 55 and over

43.4% Consumers aged 25 to 44

19.7% Consumers under age 25

Total $1.0bn

Source: IBIS World Report on the US Food Truck Industry: March 2019

Question: As a reader and person interested in a future startup or having already started a new venture, can you summarize the industry or sector you want to disrupt/compete in using ten points to do so, equivalent to those listed here?

SLAM Step 1

Unmet need(s) and which segments (including the most likely 'beach-head') experience the most pains or gains that would be alleviated by your solution?

Unmet needs are issues, frustrations or challenges that customers experience in their business or personal lives for which a better solution would either remove/lessen the relative pain or represent a significant improvement in the experience (even if they don't have a clear realization of this yet) – a gain.

Sometimes these issues are large in scale and scope or are small challenges with a very specific application to a limited group of people. Issues may also be tangible and/or known but can also be less tangible and/or not readily recognized or appreciated.

For example, some people may get migraine headaches and experience hours of literal pain and a new drug could, at least in trials perhaps, reduce this pain level and the time over which it is experienced, perhaps significantly.

Alternatively, in the less tangible category, customers were once happy to browse and shop in physical bookstores and only had minor cause to think about limitations in variety or choice, with an average of 10,000 to 15,000 books to browse in a small store perhaps only a few years ago. When Amazon came along offering a million books, at least initially, shipped to a buyer's home and at a cheaper price, they disrupted the industry so much that the vast majority of physical bookstores quickly disappeared, and Amazon continued on to disrupt other industries with their e-commerce-led solution and become a vast and multi-faceted business.

On the gain side of the equation, smartphone vehicle navigational apps like Waze and Google Maps, not only offered in-the-moment traffic predictions and journey-time indications (and reduced the 'pain' of being late considerably) but also offered the 'gain' of alternative routes that save drivers time by taking the best available route at the time.

In simple terms, customer 'pain' points can consequently be considered to be real current frustrations, difficulties and challenges (even if there is no apparent solution to them right now), while customer 'gains' can be considered to be productivity boosters or easier ways to get things done.

This pain and gain identification is just as true for Business to Business (B2B) rather than just Business to Consumer (B2C) issues, although in B2B we may need to think harder about who actually experiences the pain or gain most, which often comes down to individual people and functions in businesses, and not a business, sector or industry as a whole.

It is important to realize that spotting market/customer gaps or possible unmet needs, and the pains and potential gains that could be realized, involves an entrepreneur not only looking for them (paying attention) but having what Professor Carol Dweck at Stanford calls an open-minded attitude or what is often called having a growth-oriented mindset as opposed to a fixed one.

An open mindset is a somewhat nebulous concept but in simple terms is a self-perception or 'self-theory' that people hold about themselves. These mindsets are prevailing beliefs around subjects such as relative intelligence, the capacity to form good relationships, relative levels of competence at a variety of tasks or even how much success in life a person may get or deserve.

Where these mindsets are both negative and fixed (or largely unchanging) they can have a profoundly adverse effect on learning achievement, skill acquisition, personal professional success, and many other dimensions of life. Most importantly it may render an individual effectively blind to the issues and challenges around them and inhibit his or her ability to address it or think differently about what could be done to improve or solve the issue.

To overcome the problems of a fixed mindset, people who want to be more successful should ideally challenge all of their apparently fixed mindsets by developing a growth mindset orientation. This involves maintaining a deep love of learning in general and adopting an approach in which all problems or issues encountered in life (to which much closer attention are paid) are viewed as challenges to be overcome. In this growth-centered approach, even failures are viewed as opportunities to improve learning and skills (and to try again).

What all of this has to do with identifying unmet needs is that a growth-centered mindset is ideal in attending to the world around the entrepreneur on a day-to-day basis. In other words, it allows an individual to be mentally curious about why people do what they do and why they live with situations that are often time consuming, expensive, difficult, complex and even frustrating day in and day out. This may well be because these people have fixed mindsets about what they are dealing with and cannot easily see how a task could be done differently.

There is no formula for having a growth-centered mindset or for viewing the world in a fresh or different way. However, some of the more common approaches by successful past entrepreneurs include regularly thinking about:

- How might the situation be made simpler or involve fewer steps?
- What new analogies or metaphors could open up possibilities for change?
- How could the situation be reversed or turned upside-down?
- What waste or 'excess capacity' exists that could be utilized?
- How does nature address or even solve problems similar to this?
- How can this situation be partially or completely reframed to gain new insights?
- Who profits from the current situation, how and why (and how might this be changed as a result)?
- What unhelpful assumptions and biases may support the current approach and create gaps or unmet needs for this set of people?

What all of the above have in common is lateral thinking, or what often simply amounts to having a deep belief – however different, wild or even far-fetched it may be – that a founder holds firmly, even if few others share this belief.

For a startup, the unmet need identification task first step then is to hypothesize about the kind of obvious and less obvious issues that specific customers might have or care about a lot, and make sure that we have thought about the target customer or segment we have in mind, which seems to experience this most. This needs to be done as clearly as possible, using as much hard data and desktop research as we can, so that real and ideally face-to-face interviews with the target set of customers who appear to have this issue the most (often called the most likely 'beach-head' market) can then take place to confirm the guesses. In practical terms, the more that entrepreneurs can get close to or try to inhabit their target customer's world, the better.

To engage in effective customer discovery of unmet needs, an entrepreneur's approach needs to be patient and get into deep-listening mode as much as they can. This is no easy task for many founders so it's good to practice and get some feedback from others about how effective this approach is and then make any changes necessary for next time.

One way to think about the unmet need(s) identification challenge is to consider what a particular customer set would pay for getting something done that is difficult/frustrating/problematic today, or for which they are experiencing far too much friction. Also, on the gain side, it is worth thinking about how they would experience new value, not available to them today. In this regard, 'friction' is a helpful term that can apply to both tiny tasks that can be irritating or problematic or very significant barriers to achieving what may be a big goal for a large number of people.

Once we have identified our target customer segment, a final step here is to think about what an average person in the population might look like, both demographically and psychographically. This average 'customer persona' can then be used as a kind of avatar to focus the team's attention as they gather data.

An important point to note here is that there may appear to be many possible customer segment targets that apparently have the same broad unmet need. In such circumstances, all target segments need to be carefully and separately identified and prioritized so that the major one(s) are considered first (or become the beach-head). If more than one segment appears to be just as attractive, a new SLAM process should ideally be developed for each.

As the reader will see, each step in the SLAM diagram has at least three key and core questions that every startup founder needs to answer. For step 1 these are:

Question 1: What are the needs, pains, gains or what problems are you trying to solve? Why is now the ideal time to solve it?

Question 2: Does this problem matter at scale or is it local and/or relatively trivial?

Question 3: Who cares most about this problem/issue now or who is the target beach-head segment and buying persona (the actual 'average' person that you have in mind here)?

SLAM Step 1

Identifying the unmet needs

Hector and Maria like to be as environmentally friendly as possible and live their lives with this in mind. They invest in eco-friendly technology in the home, buy 'green' products as much as feasible, try to avoid as much plastic as they can, recycle as much as possible and drive an electric car. They also compost and grow fruit and vegetables in their small garden.

Hector and Maria have many friends who either have the same 'green' approach or aspire to do more of this. But the group of people they see embracing this approach most are younger adults between the ages of 21 and 35, who, as yet, have no or few children, do not have gardens to grow food (probably renting their home or apartment) but want to eat healthily and from sustainable sources, if they can afford it. They have an average budget of $100 each week for eating out, which must cover drinks too.

The problem at the present time is that 'green' restaurants (still a lot less than 5% of the total) are mainly in large urban centers in southern California (like Santa Monica and Pasadena, for example) but not that available in smaller centers or smaller towns and other sites. In addition, these restaurants are often expensive and are usually only partly 'green' or eco-friendly. They can also be quite expensive – a limiting factor.

Hector and Maria live in an area that has many university campuses. In Orange County alone there are 12 large colleges with six of them with over 30,000 students each. The target customer persona here, therefore, is believed to be a college student aged 18 to 22 who wants to eat lunch or dinner locally, off-campus, at least once a week and get good food that is sustainably sourced at a reasonable price. Hector and Maria are conscious that this may be an assumption on their part and even a fixed mindset so know they should spend time to learn from many sources to determine whether this is true.

SLAM Step 2

The key team (founding members including the potential CEO, CTO and CMO)

Once we have a range of unmet needs identified (this may be only one or two, but is often more like six to eight), we should not only prioritize these, from most important to least important, and then focus on not so much how these unmet needs (pains and gains) may best be solved for (which we will aim to do in step 3) but who or which people can best address the issues and develop the possible solution(s).

Although early team members are usually called founders, it is often useful to think about the skills needed to address and potentially solve the particular problem, issue or challenge that has been identified. This may be technically, operationally, financially, legally, from a marketing perspective and even in terms of leadership. In other words, the key consideration in this step is to ask what kind of knowledge and experience would be most useful to apply in these circumstances, and with this target situation and beach-head market in mind?

This does not necessarily mean industry knowledge and experience, by the way. Founders at Uber, AirBnB and DollarShave, for example, had little knowledge of the taxi, hotel, or men's grooming business or any direct experience in any of them. However, in all three of these cases, these founders had the personal experience of frustration or unmet needs and were knowledgeable and had an open attitude or adopted a growth-oriented mindset, about digging into the views of people who shared this same challenge. They were then also quick to bring in target sector experts and advisers to help them further.

The key point to remember here is that it is real people who intermediate between having to really understand the market and the customer base who are most in need and the product design or feature set that is likely to make the situation better or to improve things. Put another way, early startup founders and employees are the 'human keys' who succeed at 'picking the lock' to get to good market-product fit.

One issue to note when assembling an early stage startup team is that hiring co-founders or early team members and advisers doesn't always mean full-time people (the capacity to pay people often comes later). Several people on the startup team may often therefore work as a 'side-hustle' for weeks, months and sometimes years while doing a 9 to 5 job elsewhere.

In early stage startup (of fully employed and side-hustle individuals) will rarely give people rigid job titles because every early worker often performs multiple roles (perhaps other than the idea originator, who may be called the CEO, or entrepreneurial lead). But where there is more than one founder, others should either ideally have knowledge or experience, or be sought to join the team, who have the ability to think about at least two other key areas:

1. The first of these is someone who can consider the particular market or target segment and how demand for a product is best generated (often eventually called the Chief Marketing Officer (CMO) or Product Manager or Director).

2. Secondly, it is important to have at least one founder who can consider the technical or technology solution needed, or, sometimes, the operational path necessary to meet demand (often eventually called the Chief Technology Officer (CTO) or Chief Operations Officer (COO) early on, but quite quickly may split into very separate roles, as the startup scales).

These roles, and the people in them, may also need to change and adjust roles and responsibilities (and provide necessary leadership) as more information from customers is gathered, of course. This is particularly true when there is more than one product or service and/ or there is more than one segment or niche of the market that may need a different focus.

At this early stage titles are not that important but the ability to take initiative, be persistent, stay on track and generally hustle are critical for all early employees, not to mention the ability to work together as a team. In addition, the founders should work hard to avoid mediocrity in the hiring process. A friend or close colleague may seem like a good and familiar choice but they may not be the best person to go the extra mile that a startup always needs.

For step 2, the key questions are:

Question 1: Which people are best able to get from 'Zero to 1' or focus on creating radical rather than incremental growth and why?

Question 2: Which people have the best capability and expertise to pursue this journey towards market-product fit for this target beach-head market?

Question 3: Which advisers can best steer the startup through the 'valley of death' and why?

SLAM Step 2

The key team

At least initially, Hector and Maria are the startup founders. Their daughter Sofia is 18 years old and will start her freshman year at Cal State Fullerton in a few months' time. Daniel is now 19 years old, has finished high school and did a year at a technical college before getting a job at a local auto-body shop where he works 7 am to 3 pm from Monday to Saturday (allowing a little 'side-hustle' work perhaps in the late afternoon/evenings).

The whole family is enthusiastic about the 'green' food truck business idea and the children will pitch in as much as they can, once it gets off the ground, but don't expect it to be a 'real' job for them for some time, if ever.

In the past, Hector brought in around $6,000 a month from his job and Maria added around $3,000, but following his early retirement, Hector and Maria used some of the money to pay off their home mortgage. They believe they can live comfortably now on around $4,500 per month (with a $3,500 minimum to pay all their bills) so this is their initial profit target from their new venture.

Hector and Maria want to start with one truck to get to really know the food truck business inside and out but would like to grow this to at least five or six trucks. This means they will be looking for staff for each of these (two per truck) over time, for all six. They will also be looking for part-time help on the bookkeeping/accounting side of things and for web site and other marketing and social media outreach that will be necessary; neither of them knows much about these two areas.

Hector and Maria have two friends who they think might help them. Ron is a local Certified Practicing Accountant (or CPA) who works with a lot of small businesses, including some restaurants. Paula is an ex-entrepreneur and sold her small business a few years ago (a shopping app) and is now a startup adviser. They have both agreed to advise the couple for free for the first few weeks in return for a small parcel of shares in the business and until revenues flow and they can get paid for their contributions.

SLAM Step 3

Product or service offering and how it offers unique and specific value to each identified key segment with unmet need(s)

Although most founders will have a product or service idea they may believe is a winner, it is critical to ensure that the product or service in mind is ultimately designed to satisfy the unmet needs identified in step 1 and to offer unique and specific value to this niche or segment of customers (often called the value proposition to the target customers).

In fact, the whole SLAM process should now be completed with only this one segment in mind, so that these unmet needs are paramount, and another SLAM is completed (as necessary) for a different segment as needed.

To put this in a slightly different way, there is little or no point to building a model or solution first (often called a 'build it and they will come' or 'solution in search of a market' approach) and then seeing if it has a group of customers who want it. This can lead to considerable wasted time and money and will often mean that the features or performance needed at the earliest stages for a particular target market could be quite different and then new features have to be added or, worse, work started again).

For example, a startup may think that a new fitness machine (say a light, portable treadmill) may be attractive to practically all seniors who can't easily get to the gym. The whole product and/or service design, including size, shape, weight, electronic display, etc. would then be conceived with this very broad and by the way, largely undifferentiated segment in mind – all seniors or older adults is a big pool of very different people.

However, if we were to also think about a different segment for this product (which could be a very particular set of seniors, such as those in skilled nursing centers with a given disease state or mobility problems or physiotherapists who deal with patients with leg injuries), this switches the market segment from Business to Consumer (B2C) to Business to Business (B2B), as nursing homes and physiotherapists become the buyer, and the design of the product would need to be a little different. We'd then consequently best complete the rest of the SLAM with this alternative segment in mind.

Although it will come up later, this early customer discovery and identification of which target is most in need for what the startup is proposing will save a lot of time, cost and energy for another reason, too. By listening carefully, the product or service design feature set will be described by and prioritized by the customer, especially when they are the early adopters or buyers, and it will allow the startup team to build a draft product development roadmap for the short, medium and long term.

One last point at this third step on the SLAM diagram. While there is nothing wrong with engaging in considerable 'what if' thinking in the team (often using creative input sessions among the founders and other early team members and advisers to look for new insights) these are only guesses and are best taken to the target beach-head customers identified earlier to test these ideas.

Other than conducting face-to-face discussions, customer discovery can be done by use of surveys, focus groups or with co-creation sessions to assess whether the product or service you are thinking about might alleviate the 'pain' or create a 'gain'. However, in the vast majority of cases, we don't need and should not engage in creating the actual offering until we have this feedback, and that is what we'll discuss in the next step on the SLAM diagram.

For step 3, the key questions are:

Question 1: What MVP feature set best solves the problem(s) for the target beach-head market?

Question 2: What is defensibly unique about the proposed/actual MVP feature set?

Question 3: What is the best-prioritized product/service pipeline development strategy?

SLAM Step 3

The product and/or service offering

Hector and Maria have identified their target customer as college students and plan to concentrate on the six biggest campuses in their area, all of which are within 25 miles of their home. That means that the truck itself needs to be located on, or close to, these campuses with the permits/licenses to operate at these locations. The truck must be clean and available at two main times – from 11am till 1.30pm for the lunch rush and then again from 4.30 till 6.30pm after classes. This schedule allows for cleaning and restocking to occur in the three hours in between these shifts.

As far as offerings are concerned, Hector and Maria want to stress that Fresh-Fare is eco-friendly in an overall sense (buys locally from sustainable sources, is organic, non-GMO, composts organic waste, uses eco-friendly and/or recyclable packaging, etc.).

In terms of food offerings, Hector and Maria intend to focus on lunch and the evening mealtime during weekdays and the occasional special event on the weekend. They will offer six different salads with 10 different dressings and a choice of three types of protein (organic salmon, steak or chicken), uniquely blended fruit and vegetable juices and four different kinds of daily fresh-baked artisanal bread. Prices will be $11 for all salads, $5 for small juices, $7.50 for large juices and $1 for artisanal bread.

All juices will be supplied in recyclable cups and salads/artisanal bread on recyclable thick paper plates with bamboo forks. Dressings come in attractive tiny glass jars that can be kept or given back to Fresh-Fare that will refund 50 cents for each jar with its cap (and these will be cleaned and reused). Napkins will be made from recyclable paper.

All product offerings can be ordered and paid for in person or via a Fresh-Fare app on a smartphone and then picked up to save customers time when they want this service.

Time to pause and reflect

These first three steps of **target market**, **focused team** and **product value proposition** to the suggested beach-head market are the most important for a founder team to craft as accurately as it can. This often takes the most time to develop, with customer feedback often leading to having to make ongoing adjustments, which can lead to small product or service design changes and sometimes significant pivots.

Many startup teams short-cut the discovery effort, (by talking to very few customers or ones that are not the actual target, for example) rush this process or become frustrated with limited or contradictory feedback. However, taking weeks or even months here can build an extremely solid foundation for the business. This is because the fit between the product and the target market is fundamentally what the startup team is trying to establish, after which a startup business can attempt to sell its product or service to the one segment. If this starts to work well, meaning the the target customers really like what is being offered, the team can then begin to identify new adjunct market segments that may fit too and in which more customers are willing to pay.

The chart on the next page shows on the SLAM diagram just how important the first three steps and the nine questions that ideally should be asked and answered carefully really are. As it suggests, in combination the information assembled should create an extremely solid foundation on which to build the business. Founders should, therefore, take much more time here than they often allow.

The 3 realms of market-product fit

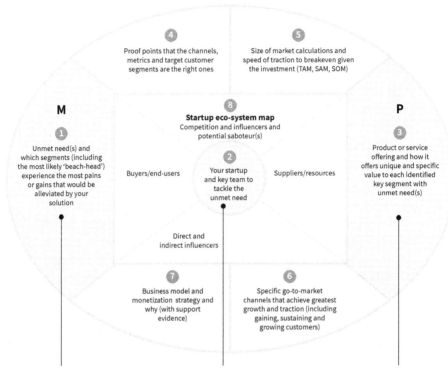

1. Unmet need(s)

Question 1: What are the needs, pains, gains or what problems are you trying to solve? Why is now the ideal time to solve it?

Question 2: Does this problem matter at scale or is it local and/or relatively trivial?

Question 3: Who cares most about this problem/issue now or who is the target beach-head segment and buying persona (the actual 'average' person that you have in mind here)?

2. Key team

Question 1: Which people are best able to get from 'Zero to 1' or focus on creating radical rather than incremental growth and why?

Question 2: Which people have the best capability and expertise to pursue this journey towards market-product fit for this target beach-head market?

Question 3: Which advisors can best steer the startup through the 'valley of death' and why?

3. Product or service offering

Question 1: What MVP feature set best solves the problem(s) for the target beach-head market?

Question 2: What is defensibly unique about the proposed/actual MVP feature set?

Question 3: What is the best-prioritized product/service pipeline development strategy?

The three areas of unmet need(s) identification (for the most pressing customer beach-head), the best team to tackle the problem and the unique product/service that will be offered (or the value proposition) are the three key elements of market-product fit. This is the 'rock' on which all successful startups should be built. If this is not strong or is not worked on enough, it will be a 'bed of sand' and may undermine medium- to long-term success of the startup.

SLAM Step 4

Proof points that the channels, metrics and target customer segments are the right ones

To reiterate, and before we take our assumptions and hypothesis 'on the road' in step 4, founders should have:

1. Clearly established the unmet needs of a particular target customer segment (the 'beach-head' and first adjunct markets);

2. Made sure the right team is focused on what is needed by the target segment; and

3. Carefully defined the product/service offering that appears to be most attractive to that beach-head market (carefully lining up particularly value propositions with each unmet need).

It is now time to start to solicit real and substantial customer input so that confirmable patterns can emerge (or not as the case may be and a minor or major pivot may be required).

Soliciting real and substantial customer input means we have to go beyond the educated guesses, the 'desktop' search efforts, internal conversations, discussions with friends and family about the idea, etc. and actually get in front of the target customer, face-to-face, and in volume.

To do this well, we need to design the experiments or hypotheses we want to test and adopt the best approach. This actively and practically aims to test what we believe without declaring these beliefs openly to our customers.

These customer discovery conversations are not a pitch conversation where the startup founder promotes or describes the product or service and asks the customer what he or she thinks about it, but a listening-centered conversation. This should, therefore, be a genuine two-way discussion in which information is gently solicited about the apparent unmet need(s) and whether or not it is indeed real or pressing, how significant it is, and how he or she may be practically dealing with it on a day-to-day basis. Of course, the customer may be

ing about his or her issue/challenge or using a workaround

e needs to be taken in these discovery conversations to avoid ~~pro~~ ng any early stage or prototype solutions or an early product and, just as it would be in a court of law, to avoid leading the witness or steering the target customer to simply confirm our pre-determined ideas or solutions we believe will be fantastic. If we fall into this trap, we will only get or not get confirmations of our hypotheses and fail to abstract new information between the lines.

This open and generally-focused feedback, especially when it is collected from many target customers (at least 30 per segment and over 100 is preferred), will ultimately provide proof points that the customer segment in mind appears to be a valid one. In most circumstances, the feedback should also offer rich information that there is a possible way to reach these customers, through a market channel that is likely to be relevant and potentially successful (including the unit economics or drivers of value which are most important in these situations).

If this proof of concept or confirmation of the 'We believe' statements is not forthcoming, it is time to either look at a different segment or to think about how the product or service may need to be changed or modified to be deemed to be valuable or wanted. It may be that these changes can be considered and acted upon quickly but in other cases, these may be adaptations or changes for later (or what will become a product/service development roadmap).

Finally, a quick point about customer discovery versus customer research.

In the most basic of terms, customer discovery is focused upon talking with target customers without suggesting a solution (even if founders think they have a good one). The aim here is to dig into how target customers think about the broad category that a startup is focused on, and then to listen to what 'pain' it brings in real and tangible terms or listening to what customers might possibly 'gain' if the pain were to diminish substantially or even disappear, or completely new solutions were possibly available.

Customer or market research, on the other hand, mostly leads with a prototype, drawing, sketch, product or service description, etc. and then asks customers to offer input and comment. This can be conducted by formal surveys or by assembling a focus group or a set of target customers. This approach tends to constrain customer thinking to the proposed solution and providing input on how it is best deployed and pointing out any possible shortfalls or problems these target customers see or identify.

Both customer discovery and research are often necessary to help hone a product or service but should be carried out separately and ideally in sequence with discovery first.

To keep reinforcing the point, in both cases, the more intelligent questions we ask of our target customers, at scale, the more we de-risk our future product or service design efforts and create a solution that is likely to be genuinely valued. Always remember, however, that we need to be ready to be potentially wrong about our assumptions, and make the necessary changes when we are.

For step 4, the key questions are:

Question 1: What key assumptions of ours are we testing with customers (including what do we believe)?

Question 2: What best questions do we ask of customers without 'leading the witness'?

Question 3: How will we best assess the feedback we collect and best develop measures of future success?

SLAM Step 4

Testing the hypotheses with customers

Despite general data gathering, none of the Hector and Maria's friends and family have been in the food truck business and few in the restaurant business and even the few food truck owners' feedback has only been incidental and casual. Hector and Maria know they have to talk with real customers in their target market (in this case college students and staff) and test as many of their assumptions, beliefs, and hypotheses as they can. Results from their research with about 100 people are summarized in the table below.

Assumption/hypothesis	Most common response obtained
College students aged 18 to 22 might prefer to eat at a conveniently located 'green' food truck, up to twice a week.	Broadly confirmed but people like to go to a food truck with a friend. Customers may visit up to 3 times a week if the fare is varied, good quality and service is quick.
Target customer is willing to pay $10 to $12 for a meal.	Targets customers will pay up to $12 for salads and $8 for juices.
Target customer would value the food truck being available for up to two hours at lunch and same at dinner time.	Confirmed but lunchtime and fast service are most critical to 75% of the population. Dinner service would be popular but so would a breakfast service.
Target customer would value eco-friendly ingredients.	Over 65% of this target said they would value 'green' food and true eco-friendliness and efforts to be sustainable.
Target customer wants a variety of fresh salad options.	Confirmed – these salads should look good, taste good and be locally sourced and fresh.
Target customer wants a variety of fruit/veg juices.	Confirmed but 50% asked if organic protein powders could also be available.
Target customer may order food via an app.	70% of this population said they might order via the app to save time.

SLAM Step 5

Size of market calculations and speed of traction to breakeven given the investment (TAM, SAM, SOM)

Size of market estimates can be generally guessed at with a little research, at a very early stage, once a startup has validated that it seems to have reasonable market-product fit. However, it is also important to see whether or not the potential for revenue is high enough to justify further effort and the capital needed is sufficient to overcome failure risks.

It is equally important to identify how much traction with customers is likely to occur, or how much scale may be needed in order to grow quickly enough, given the competitive threats along the way, and eventually achieve fiscal break-even, or reach the point at which revenues are greater than expenses. This is particularly critical where a market is highly complex, has a lot of regulation or perhaps is one in which a startup will need to work hard to protect its intellectual property (with strong trademarks, trade secrets or patents for instance).

One well-established way to do this market-sizing is to calculate the Total Addressable Market (TAM), Serviceable Addressable Market (SAM), and Serviceable Obtainable Market (SOM).

The TAM is the whole universe of possible buyers. This does not mean everyone on the planet. It means anyone who is capable of buying the product or service in total in the target segment identified.

The SAM is usually the market that a startup can actually reach – this may be a narrower geography or part of the possible buying population – such as all men or all women only.

Finally, the SOM is the realistic market of possible buying customers in the segment that can be practically reached with the resources available to the startup, such as numbers of sales staff available to make calls, for instance.

For example, a mobile software application, which teaches better tennis techniques with videos, may have a TAM of all the existing people who play tennis recreationally in the world.

The SAM, on the other hand, is what the startup might practically reach for its tennis coaching videos. In this instance, this may be constrained by geography (the USA) and those people who own an Android mobile phone (as the app may only be available in this format initially). The SOM, in this instance, may be much more local (only in Texas, for instance) and beginners already using video-based apps on their phone, for example.

The TAM, SAM, and SOM for a customer segment can be calculated in two ways:

- Firstly this is as a 'top-down' exercise, completed largely by desktop research online and relying on published data about the target sector.

- The second way is to do this is 'bottom-up'. This way, the SOM is tackled first and estimates what revenues a startup can realistically reach in a fixed timeframe, say one year, with a given marketing spend or sales team and then extends to the SAM by looking at how much the startup can be grown or scaled up over say three years, and how much further this might reach.

- Finally, we calculate the TAM by thinking about how much of the total market might be captured in say a five-year period, which might now reach nationally or internationally.

By conducting this market sizing exercise, top-down and bottom-up, we can finally compare the findings and assess how well they seem to accord with one another and if not, why not. We will also have usually formed a rudimentary view at this step of how the target market operates, who operates within it and with what market share, and how relatively difficult it is to gain a foothold and gain future traction.

One issue to note in conducting both a top-down or bottom-up market sizing exercise is that this is likely to be a 'best-guess' or credible estimate. Given this, the key is then is to determine whether or not the opportunity that is presented is sufficiently large and worth pursuing.

In general, the results of all of this market-sizing effort will typically fall into three categories:

1. The target market is small (in numbers of customers and/or possible revenues to be earned) and it either may not be viable to launch the business in this market or it may only be small (often called a 'lifestyle' business).

2. The target market is attractive but not large and may have access difficulties (such as lots of competition or considerable regulations to deal with). In this situation, startups have to think about whether the effort, capital and time to gain traction is worth the effort.

3. The target market is very large and/or attractive. This usually means that the market is highly accessible and disruptable and there is outstanding revenue and profit earning potential.

For step 5, the key questions are:

Question 1: How big is the total addressable market and is it big enough?

Question 2: How big is the serviceable addressable market, and why?

Question 3: How big is the serviceable obtainable market and why, and can we validate this top down and bottom up?

SLAM Step 5

Sizing the market

Hector and Maria know that the overall food truck business in the US generates $1B in revenue and a truck can earn anywhere from $50,000 to $450,000 each in annual sales with profitability at 5% to 20%. However, the southern California market is a little different and more critical for them to evaluate. There are 900 large food trucks in Southern California, each with average revenues of $300,000, making an estimated total revenue of $270M/year.

This $270M then is Fresh-Fare's Total Addressable Market or top-down TAM in the current Food Truck market, but they also believe they can potentially steal away some business from college cafeterias, local coffee shops, as well as real dine-in restaurants to add to this – perhaps by 10%.

As far as Fresh-Fare's Serviceable Obtainable Market or SOM is concerned, they believe this can be restricted to Orange County (OC) only in the first few years, and this reduces food truck numbers to just 90 in county and 30 that will travel in occasionally from outside the county. They estimate SAM revenues to be $34 million.

Finally, Fresh-Fare's Serviceable Addressable Market or SAM will be six OC college campuses for the first two to three years and then all 12 thereafter when they have more trucks. In addition, they plan to supply 35 weekend special events in the county. Hector and Maria estimate that the SOM is $7.5 million in revenue.

When Hector and Maria do a bottom-up market sizing exercise, they realize that one truck and two people with each can service 100 covers at lunchtime and 50 in the evening and another 50 on their 35 weekend days. At their proposed $9 average price (across salads, juices, and artisanal bread) this means revenues of $354,000 per truck per year and $2.1 million, at year 5, if they have six trucks. This would mean that Fresh-Fare would have 25% to 30% of the college campus food truck market at year 5. This seems a little aggressive and Maria suggests that maybe 5 food trucks or one a year added is a better target for Fresh-Fare.

SLAM Step 6

Specific go-to-market channels that achieve greatest growth and traction (including gaining, sustaining and growing customers)

It is customer discovery and feedback that will determine exactly which market(s) to target initially and then determine the sales channels that are likely to be best in order to reach the individuals (and ideally the buyers or consumers) in this target segment.

This go-to-market step is all about making educated guesses about the type of market the startup is trying to enter and which channels appear to be most applicable to both attract target customers and then retain and grow more.

There are essentially three types of markets that a startup enters:

1. An existing and well-defined market with lots of competition;

2. A niche market, which often has less competition and is open to some change or what is often called 're-segmentation'; and

3. A brand new market, where there is no apparent competition and customers may have never seen a product or service like the one the startup provides before (for example, the Apple iPhone, Google Home or Amazon Alexa).

All three of these markets need a different go-to-market strategy, as it does a consideration of the channels that will create early growth or traction.

For bigger companies, developing a marketing strategy is easier to do as they have an established brand and often a larger budget. However, for the startup, they often have limited cash, so spending wisely and picking a small number of great channels is crucial. Good marketing may be oxygen for a startup business but founders need to know where to target getting it. It should be noted that more startup funding is 'wasted' in mis-targeted marketing and sales effort that in all other areas combined.

A further point to note in this step is that although growth and traction are similar concepts, they are not quite the same thing.

Growth is usually adding more customers or increasing the volume of the customer base, while traction is getting to new and existing customers. More importantly, getting customers to come back again and again or buy more (spending more or buying more frequently is crucial). This is often also referred to as customer engagement and/or retention, and startups need to know which marketing channels best achieve this.

A marketing channel is a way for customers to be reached and includes many possibilities such as direct sales, advertising, public relations, conferences, and trade shows, affiliate programs, Search Engine Optimization (SEO) and Search Engine Management (SEM), the use of email, the use of various social media channels and many others.

Usually, a startup has only so much bandwidth and capital to put money into each marketing channel, so great care needs to be taken to identify the ones that are most likely to be effective or successful given the product/service and the target customer buyer.

A useful rule-of-thumb here is that most startups cannot afford to be in more than three marketing channels early on and spending on channel one (the best-estimated converter) will be around 65%, spending on the second channel (second best converter) will be 25% and spending on the third channel will be 10%. These may vary from business to business but are useful ways for a startup to plan and allocate time and resources.

A startup must consequently choose the two or three channels which are likely to be most successful as early as possible and switch to others if they prove to be not as effective as first thought, or when necessary. The proving or testing of these early marketing efforts often distinguishes a focused and serious startup in the eyes of investors.

While having a robust strategy to gain customers is crucial, every startup needs to be careful ensure that the customers they win (early adopters and pioneers perhaps) are kept happy or sustained. This usually means having a tangible retention plan to make sure they remain satisfied and are not forgotten as soon as they are acquired. In addition, startups should have a customer growth strategy, often leveraging existing customers to help find and refer new ones, which may even involve having a new customer incentive plan.

Although we will talk about it more on the GRAND side of the map, it is important for all startups to at least begin to consider their cost of customer acquisition (COCA) and long-term customer value equation (LTV). This should be done in an overall sense but also by selected channel, making sure that customer 'churn' is factored in too.(as this can mean that a startup may have to work much harder, when the percentage is high).

Both of these calculations are helpful in determining whether a marketing channel can deliver its expected value (and, if not, to stop using that channel and find a better converting one).

For step 6, the key questions are:

Question 1: Which major marketing channels best reach the target beach-head customers and why?

Question 2: What is the priority order of the best marketing channels and how much money can/should we spend in each to maximize customer acquisition?

Question 3: How will we best test each channel and change tactics based on our relative success and ensure have sound acquisition, retention and growth plans?

SLAM Step 6

Go-to-market strategies

Because they are targeting mainly college campuses, especially early on, Hector and Maria talked to their own children about how to best reach or market to them and then supplemented this with lots of questions of many students in different years and studying for different classes. They found that most students paid the greatest attention to what their peers said first and then what was said on social media apps second and then responded to incentives third. Other marketing methods also mentioned, but not so popular, were direct advertising on college noticeboards, 'Influencer' marketing and special promotional events.

Because almost every student seemed to have a smartphone, Hector and Maria built the Fresh-Fare website to be mobile friendly and developed an app, both appealing and easy to use, on both IOS and Android platforms. This allowed quick menu browsing, simple ordering ahead of time, a loyalty scheme to join, with the ability get discounts and deals and the functionality to get 'push notifications' when specials were announced. They also added functionality to let customers post comments and reviews 'in-app' and to easily add these to other popular platforms, if they wished.

Hector and Maria spent most of their online advertising budget on Instagram and also identified students with the most followers on this platform and asked them to post reviews on Fresh-Fare eating experiences after being given 50% off vouchers to try it out. Twitter was also used extensively to alert students that the truck was there each day and to tell weekend target customers where the truck would be and when. Hector and Maria also made sure that they got as many good reviews on YELP as possible.

Hector and Maria spent considerable time and attention on the Fresh-Fare brand and how the business is eco-friendly and the food is farm-fresh, organic and locally sourced. A series of postcards, banners and door hangers were designed and printed for a variety of advertising locations and channels, including common area and college departmental notice boards.

SLAM Step 7

Business model and monetization strategy and why (with support evidence)

Many startup founders believe that their product and service simply needs to be priced and then offered to see if this works or is readily accepted by target customers. This kind of pricing is often created with too little thought or calculation, or is based on either a cost-plus foundation or by using a comparison to the deemed competitive offerings in the market. This crude approach often leads to a sub-optimal outcome and a shift to getting a customer to pay to overcome a pain point or pay to realize a significant gain is likely to be much more effective.

There are many ways to invite customers to think about removing a pain point or to receive a tangible gain. Simple examples of drivers might be less time to complete a project or task is taken or less effort in getting work done is realized, and then determining the value-add as a result.

This effort to identify the real value a product or service offers and then coming up with the right or best pricing system is called determining the most appropriate business model or which 'monetization model' is likely to work best (and being able to say why this is the case).

The different kinds of business or monetization models include rental systems, leasing, subscription, the razor/razor blade model and many pricing approaches ('below the competition', 'for volume', etc.).

While all pricing models (we hope) monetize the startup in some way, each one needs to be thought through carefully to ensure that it is not a barrier (and doesn't just add a margin to costs or slightly undercut a competitive offering, for example). This is simply because a price without also conveying the value it brings will simply fail in most cases.

As a result, startups should conduct considerable research on the value that the product or service brings, with as much supporting evidence as possible as to why this is likely to be effective and acceptable to customers, something that should be tested fully in the discovery process, of course.

One other apparently small consideration that it is worth every startup founder thinking about at this monetization step is whatever price you set for the product or service this needs to achieve two consistency ends:

1. The sales and go-to-market strategy must be able to deliver the volume of 'units' needed to hit the monthly and yearly targets set (this will clearly be many more units for a low priced product/ service than a high priced one).

2. The overall financial projections should reflect this 'price times volume' equation. In other words, revenues when divided by average unit prices provide the same target that the go-to-market plan assumes. We will cover the financial projections in more detail on the GRAND diagram later in this book.

One key point to note here is that using distribution partners may substantially change the business model and monetization economics, mainly because they will often have their own internal overheads to recover and target margins to make. This means that a distribution partner may be initially attractive because it appears to lower the cost of customer acquisition for a startup but may mean that the net price they are subsequently willing to pay to the startup is relatively low (and fail to cover the full costs of maintaining the relationship).

For step 7, the key questions are:

Question 1: How much value do we create for customers and why?

Question 2: What business or monetization model best fits the strategy for each target market(s)?

Question 3: What is our cost of customer acquisition (COCA) and long-term value (LTV) created for our target beach-head customers?

SLAM Step 7

The business model and monetization

At one level the Fresh-Fare business model is extremely simple: sell environmentally friendly, organic and sustainable food from their truck(s) which is easy to access (local) and little more expensive than fast-food, but a lot cheaper (at least 50%) than a restaurant. They do this at two major times (both lunch and at evening mealtime) and they could, of course, extend this further to breakfast, for example.

Hector and Maria have constrained their ways of monetizing, especially in the early years, largely to college campuses on weekdays and special local events on weekends. It may, therefore, pay for them to split up their possible revenue streams for not only these different customer groups but according to the times that they offer service (and they could get even more granular if they wished). For example, Hector and Maria could build a table such as the one below. The analysis suggests that annual revenues per truck are $416,150 with 59% of this revenue coming from salads.

Customer group/ days per annum	Organic eggs $5 for 2	Artisanal bread $3	Juices $6	Salads $10	Other $2
College weekday breakfast x 250	x 30 = $150	x 20 = $60	x 40 = $240	x 5 = $50	x 10 = $20
College weekday lunch x 250	x 5 = $25	x 10 = $30	x 20 = $120	x 50 = $500	x 10 = $20
College weekday evening meal x 250	x 2 = $10	x 5 = $15	x 3 = $18	x 25 = $250	x 10 = $20
Weekend day event lunch x 50	x 5 = $25	x 15 = $45	x 5 = $30	x 30 = $300	x 5 = $10
Weekend event evening meal x 50	x 30 = $15	x 10 = $30	x 3 = $18	x 20 = $200	x 5 = $10
Total	x 45 = $225	x 60 = $180	x 71 = $270	x 120 = $1,200	x 40 = $48

SLAM Step 8

Start-up eco-system map: (a) Competition and potential saboteur(s), (b) Buyers/end-users, (c) Suppliers/resources, (d) Direct and indirect influencers

The final step of the SLAM diagram involves thinking about what existing 'eco-system' this particular startup will compete in when trying to sell to customers, and how the various players in it might respond both positively and negatively.

The startup founders will have already thought about the type of market it intends to enter but now must be much more granular in their thinking about:

(a) Competition and potential saboteur(s)

Competitive offerings may be direct or indirect (or existing businesses that could easily pivot into your market segment or emulate your product/service features).

Many startups believe that they do not really have competitors, as they are either relatively unique or that their suite or 'bundle' of offerings is very different from anyone else. However, a better way to think about competitors is to focus on who is attempting to reduce or eliminate the unmet needs or pain points for these target customers. With this perspective, many more possible competitors are likely to be worth reviewing.

While some competitors may be obvious in a given area, some will be more difficult to discover. Founders should, therefore, spend time searching and reviewing industry databases, directories and lists, checking out web sites (e.g. Hoovers, Bloomberg, Crunchbase, Owler) and asking questions during the customer discovery process to see who people most identify with.

These competitors should be listed and evaluated in terms of what each competitor currently offers, even in terms of their published feature set, and pricing, and why the startup's solution is tangibly better. This step also includes the identification of any potential saboteurs or eco-system participants who could possibly resist or threaten or even sabotage the startup's market entry.

(b) Buyers/end-users

A buyer of a startup's product or service can take many forms and will vary depending on whether the startup is B2B- or B2C-focused (and other variants including B2B2C or Business to Government (B2G) for example).

An end-consumer may also be a buyer, but sometimes there are 'economic buyers' who are also intermediaries (parents, teachers, managers, purchasing officers, etc.).

Each of these buyer/end-users need to be listed and considered carefully in terms of how commonplace this buying person is across the chosen target sector.

In many cases, especially when the target beach-head buying customer has been identified and validated, a startup will develop a detailed 'persona' for this person or a profile which describes on average who they are likely to be and how they are likely to buy.

Care also needs to be taken here to note when products or services are bought by a buying team or group of people that must sign off on a purchase. This is particularly common in larger-scale companies and both B2B and B2G situations.

(c) Suppliers/resources

Suppliers are all those people in the possible supply chain that can help the startup get to market. These may be OEMs (original equipment manufacturers), developers, distributors, resellers, IP attorneys or even marketers, for instance.

Whatever the startup's product or service, suppliers and other support resources entities need to be specifically identified as potential alliances or partners in the future journey. In other words, suppliers can often be extremely helpful to the new startup venture in reaching its target customers, especially when the partnership can deliver clearly identified 'win–win' gains for both parties. The economic impact of each possible partnership can then be calculated.

(d) Direct and indirect influencers

An influencer is not usually a buyer but is someone who encourages others to buy.

These may be direct influencers who often, at least partially, directly benefit from the startup's success, or indirect influencers, who may have deep knowledge about the target segment in question and believe that solving for its 'pains and gains' is worthy (and may, therefore, provide support on the right basis).

The right basis may range from simply liking what the startup is doing and a resultant willingness to promote it (write about the startup in a blog post or local newspaper/magazine, interview the founders on a radio show etc.) to offering direct incentives to 'push' the startup's product to the influencer's audience (such as free or cheaper product).

Once again, the first eco-system described or drawn on the SLAM diagram is unlikely to be the last and customer discovery will probably both change it and enhance it over time as more and more information is gathered about all four of the above categories.

For step 8, the key questions are:

Question 1: How do we best design our startup to make a successful entry into the existing business eco-system and landscape?

Question 2: How should we best evaluate and out-strip our perceived direct and indirect competition and saboteurs?

Question 3: Who are our best/most optimal suppliers and influencers to maximize success and build defensible barriers to entry (create as near a monopoly as we can)?

SLAM Step 8

Entering the existing business eco-system

The food truck industry has been steadily growing over the past 10 years or so and is predicted to grow further in the future. This means that there is lots of competition now and much more to come. In addition, by their very nature, food trucks are mobile so as Hector and Maria do well in a market, other food trucks can come into their space (even by traveling from outside Orange County) and compete directly and impact daily revenues dramatically. Furthermore, local restaurants (fast and medium food and fine dining) are unlikely to stand still and will change strategies to compete and try to steal back any business lost. Fresh-Fare, therefore, needs to map the eco-system carefully.

The best way for Hector and Maria to map the business eco-system is to list all of the types of customers (in this case they are a direct-to-consumer offering on one side and all the eco-friendly food and packaging and other suppliers to their business on the other). They should then identify direct (D) and indirect (I) competitors and then who are likely to be positive or helpful influencers in their space. The chart overleaf might be one that they draw as a first draft.

This chart can be drawn with even more detail if Fresh-Fare wants to do so, and they may also start to draw lines between entities both in terms of product, service and workflow and in terms of the typical flow of money (revenue and net profits). In addition, Fresh-Fare could begin to think more deeply about how to deal with particularly competitors, customer groups and suppliers or even individual influencers (such as a specific local journalist that writes about good local food).

Business eco-system for the Fresh-Fare food truck startup

COMPETITORS

Other food trucks	Fast food restaurants	Campus commissary
Coffee shops	Fine food restaurants	Service stations

SUPPLIERS (D)

(I)

Farms and market gardens
Organic bread bakers
Packaging and utensil suppliers
Truck suppliers and maintenance

FRESH-FARE

CUSTOMERS

College students
College teachers, staff, support
Orange County conferences
Music events
Wedding events

Food writers	Food truck bloggers	Wedding bloggers
Student influencers	Campus newswriters	Local event writers

INFLUENCERS

46

SLAM summary

If a startup has maintained a solid focus and made sure that their information is based on real and candid input, ideally from face-to-face discovery-centered discussions with carefully identified target customers, by this point they should have gathered information on all eight steps below:

1. The unmet need(s) and which segments (including the most likely beach-head) experience the most pains or gains that would be alleviated by the proposed solution.

2. The key team (founding members including the potential CEO, CTO, and CMO) and any key advisers that can open up or bring about success in the target market.

3. The product or service offering and how it offers unique and specific value to each identified key segment with the unmet need(s).

4. Proof points that the channels, metrics and target customer segments are the right ones.

5. Size of market calculations and speed of traction to breakeven given the investment (TAM, SAM, SOM).

6. Specific go-to-market channels that can achieve greatest growth and traction (including gaining, sustaining and growing customers).

7. Business model and monetization strategy and why (with support evidence and cost of customer acquisition and long-term value equations).

8. Start-up eco-system map: (a) Competition and potential saboteur(s), (b) Buyers/end-users, (c) Suppliers/resources, (d) Direct and indirect influencers.

Most importantly of all, the startup should also have realized that, as information is gathered at each step, it may act to change the views formed at earlier steps or cause minor or major 'pivots'. This is healthy iteration and means that the startup is both de-risking the business going forward and pushing the great entrepreneurship holy grail – market-product fit.

An example of what the Fresh-Fare SLAM diagram could look like is shown opposite. Don't forget, this is only summary information and in ideal circumstances founders should have much more detailed back-up notes and data gathered at every step separately.

At the end of the SLAM process the startup should have a choice or decision to make: Do we stop completely? Do we make some major adjustments and dig into a new or different SLAM process? or Do we go forward as we have a lot of confidence that we have something good here? If it's the latter, it's time to turn the diagram over and go to the GRAND diagram, where you will be digging in further and, most of all, focusing on the many execution issues that a startup must manage well.

SLAM for Fresh-Fare

M

① Customers (mainly college students in OC) want:
- Fresh food
- Healthy food
- Tasty food
- Quality food
- Sustainably sourced
- Reasonably priced
- Easily accessed
- Quickly served
- Variety of options
- Authentic in every way

④ The 'I believe' hypothesis:
- Millennials in particular are interested in eco-friendly, sustainably-sourced food
- Millennials want healthy food options
- Customers want reasonable prices
- Different food trucks would be attractive

⑤ TAM, SAM and SOM:
- The TAM is $270 million
- The SAM is $34 million
- The SOM is $7 million
- The college market is hugely unserved in OC right now

P

③ Products/services:
- 1 'green' food truck growing to a total of 6 food trucks within 5 years
- Locally sourced fresh and healthy food
- Core focus on multiple tasty fresh salads with great healthy dressings
- Added food items like organic eggs and artisinal bread
- Supplemented by great fruit and veg juices
- made to order
- All served quickly

⑧ Competition: other local food trucks, on-campus cafeteria and local fast food restaurants and coffee shops

②

Key team:
Initially Hector and Maria + 2 kids PT + 2 advisors

Buyers/end-users:
- College students aged 18 to 22 mainly
- Other local foot traffic
- Weekend event attendees

Direct and indirect influencers:
- Students, food truck and food bloggers, local newspapers, local radio

Suppliers/resources:
- Food suppliers
- Drink suppliers
- Consumable suppliers
- Truck maintainers

⑥ Go-to-market channels:
- Considerable PR to launch
- Build an email list
- Heavy use of social media
- Direct marketing
- Referral scheme
- Discounts and vouchers

⑦ Business model:
- Clear pricing for 4 'green' and/or organic food options and 2 drink options
- Park near college campuses
- Attend weekend events
- Serve quickly

Decision-making options when the SLAM process is complete

Whether it has taken weeks, months or sometimes even longer to complete the SLAM process, with lots of iterations and changes on it, as more information is gathered, there is a point at which the startup's founders can say it is complete.

'Complete' is something of a strange term as the market keeps changing over time and sometimes very quickly. However, founders will typically know when this particular diagram has enough information to now make a decision going forward and this ultimately boils down to three possibilities:

1. We have not proved our assumptions and hypotheses or we have uncovered one or more significant reasons why this startup, in its current form should not go forward.

2. We have encountered some confirmation of assumptions and hypotheses but others have not been confirmed and we need to gather more data or need to investigate further in order to be confident going forward.

3. Our assumptions and hypotheses have been broadly confirmed and we are confident that this startup has a real and immediate opportunity to launch, grow and become profitable within a reasonable timeframe.

If the outcome is the first of the above, the best approach is often to completely pause all effort and have the entire startup team (and certainly the founders) discuss whether they want to cease all efforts or work towards a new set of customers and/or hypotheses (and they should estimate the time and resources they have available to do this). This is a time for total honesty and not for trying to 'spin' the data in a different way so as to keep going in the same direction. Many startups do this for weeks, months and years, only to ultimately fail and sometimes greatly frustrate their investors in doing so.

If the outcome is the second one above, more work clearly needs to be done and the SLAM diagram is an excellent vehicle to assess where the gaps or problems might lie and what changes may need to be made, including different assumptions, target customer segments, and product/service value propositions.

Founders should naturally think about time and resources in revisiting the SLAM diagram rigorously and in detail but also realize that this is a low-cost way of carefully validating their startup ideas and 'de-risking' their venture.

Finally, if the decision is the third of these above, it's time to press on with speed and urgency (so others don't jump in more quickly) and look now at the GRAND diagram.

3 forward options

The 8 steps of the GRAND process

The SLAM process has a reverse side to it – the GRAND (Goal, Results, Action Navigational Device) diagram as shown on the next page. This is intended to be the startup execution template and drafted only when the SLAM process has been thoroughly tested by customer discovery, which will certainly take weeks and often can take many months. This will have revealed whether or not, with adjustments or 'pivots', this startup is worthy of scaling and now subject to detailed execution planning effort.

The GRAND diagram includes more detail (and limited space to summarize findings) in terms of a business launch or scaling timeframe, new team members to be potentially hired and pricing plans, including much more detailed cost of customer acquisition (COCA), and long-term value calculations (LTV). The diagram also prompts for how much capital may need to be raised and how it should be spent, including how much of it on any resources or necessary business infrastructure

The GRAND diagram also includes how a minimal viable product (MVP) should best be deployed with the possible product or service roadmap features to be potentially added over time. Finally, in the center are prompts to develop all the necessary financial projections for the business, usually over a five-year period, including the major assumptions upon which these figures are based.

Let's now describe each of the eight steps in a little more detail.

The Goal, Results, Action Navigational Device (GRAND)

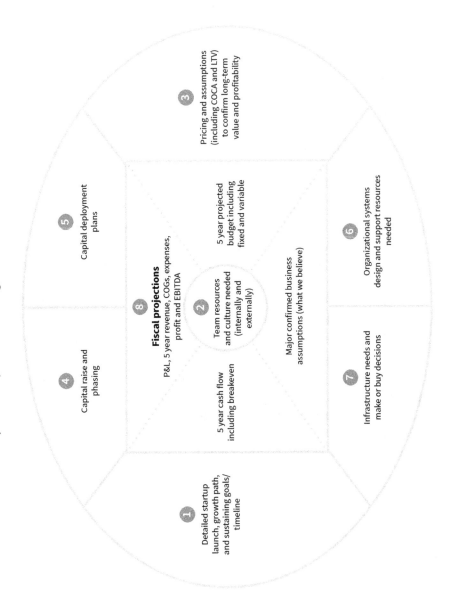

3 Pricing and assumptions (including COCA and LTV) to confirm long-term value and profitability

5 Capital deployment plans

Fiscal projections
P&L, 5 year revenue, COGs, expenses, profit and EBITDA

8

2 Team resources and culture needed (internally and externally)

5 year projected budget including fixed and variable

4 Capital raise and phasing

5 year cash flow including breakeven

Major confirmed business assumptions (what we believe)

6 Organizational systems design and support resources needed

1 Detailed startup launch, growth path, and sustaining goals/ timeline

7 Infrastructure needs and make or buy decisions

GRAND Step 1

Detailed startup launch, growth path and sustaining goals/ timeline

While a startup founder or team may have been operating together in close proximity or remotely and part-time and/or full-time for weeks, months or sometimes even years, working on customer discovery and validation, a time arises when a decision to fully and often publicly launch in earnest is taken and a detailed growth plan needs to be put in place.

This is different from prior efforts because the startup has been deemed to be on solid footing and is now ready for 'primetime'. Primetime here often means raising much more capital (which could be loans, angel or venture capital) and pushing the business into a significantly higher gear with additional people being recruited and held accountable for efforts and results.

Although every startup will be different in its approach, the first task is to move the emphasis away from idea validation and primarily listening to customer feedback (although this should never be abandoned, of course) to building the product or service in earnest and at scale, or offering a value proposition, which is deemed to be worthy and for which customers are willing to pay.

In basic terms, this new focus involves offering the minimal viable proposition (MVP) to beach-head customers who said they would like to be pioneers or early adopters and getting them to influence others to join them.

These early pioneers will often be enthusiastic users but will also be quick to offer feedback about what additional product/service roadmap features they would like to see developed and offered in the future. This can be very useful input, but only if the needs are widely corroborated and not a one-off request. Put another way, the major early goal is to get customers to pay for the most basic version of a product or service that alleviates a pain point or creates a gain, and then only add additional features when further customer payment is likely to be possible.

The key here is often to engage in much more 'push marketing' of the product or service and make sales regularly and then listen to user feedback. This is why a launch or re-launch with targeted public relations efforts, press releases, use of social media and other marketing tactics can be so useful here, as it helps to flip the culture from its design-first focus to a sales-first focus.

At this point, a startup is likely to pay very close attention to any need for a major change in direction or an 'infection point' that it encounters as it attempts to grow. Examples of this could be situations such as expanding into a new segment or market, launching a completely new product or service and dealing with a new and perhaps very aggressive competitor as the startup becomes more visible and known in the market.

As part of the re-launch planning, the startup management team should be thinking about switching into MVP sales mode and calculating how much growth they should expect or what sales or revenue trajectory they can achieve. For a tangible product, this is important for manufacturing and shipment planning, but even for a less tangible product like software, for example, it creates useful targets for which the whole startup team can aim.

One of the best ways to support a growth trajectory is to establish a few key metrics, which help measure how much input or work is necessary to get to the target sales levels each day, week, or month. According to the type of startup, this will change for each team.

For example, a marketing team will want to measure people attracted to the top of the 'sales funnel' or level of product/service demand. A sales team may want to measure number of product/service demonstrations or meetings. A development/operations team may want to measure the number of features finished/successfully tested and made available (often measured in user stories completed and 'sprints').

The metrics selected are often summarized across a startup/early stage company as OKRs (Objectives and Key Results) and they are typically a visual summary of what has been agreed as the major measures for all to see and discuss. This helps to establish very specific goals, monthly and/or quarterly to achieve. These can then be disseminated to the whole team and reset or adjusted when a target has been met and a new one is needed. Simple and meaningful OKRs can take time and considerable founder team effort to set up well. However, once they are established, they can be extremely effective drivers of ongoing performance.

Finally, at this step, the founder(s) should set clear goals and targets around growth and the desired level of traction (and the timelines that matter to reach those targets whether they are weekly, monthly, quarterly or longer). This should not be an arbitrary exercise in just selecting a target randomly or on a wishful basis. It should be based on a realistic estimate of what can actually be achieved on a practical basis by the marketing and sales team in particular.

Factors that will play into this goal and target-setting effort, therefore, are the number of people a startup has focused on getting new customers, spending in various marketing channels and the capacity to quickly learn from both successes and failures. It may also depend on a few easy-to-understand metrics on people's outreach efforts such as the number of emails sent, calls made or demonstrations made of the product or service.

As you will see, just as it was for the SLAM process, each step in the GRAND process has at three core questions that every startup founder needs to answer. For step 1, these are:

Question 1: In what way(s) do we launch or re-launch the startup with our newly established confidence that our journey towards product-market fit is on track?

Question 2: How do we best calculate our growth trajectory and the metrics/OKRs that will best track it with appropriate milestones to reach/aim for?

Question 3: What best growth and traction goals should we establish and then how do we best disseminate them to the team?

GRAND Step 1

Full launch and growth path planning

Having decided their SLAM discovery was very positive and having bought one secondhand food truck, at this stage, Fresh-Fare is ready to launch in earnest. There are several fairly clear steps for Hector and Maria to do including:

1. Ensuring that they have enough working capital to pay for everything. In a cash business like this, there are fewer issues but there should still be a 'float' and someone should be ensuring that proceeds are taken to the bank and deposited every day.

2. Making sure they have all food truck design and alterations complete, including colors, branding and desired visual factors.

3. Ordering all supplies needed for launch (for the day, week, month, etc.). This will include all food and drink ingredients, and cleaning supplies, packaging supplies, other consumables and truck running supplies.

4. Making sure that the key daily and weekly measures of success are recorded.

5. Making sure that staff knows what they need to do, hour-by-hour, day-by-day and week-by-week. As this is Hector and Maria initially, they may think they know, but how tasks are split up and who is accountable needs careful orchestration.

6. Ensuring that customers know when they will be close by and open (both ahead of time and on the day).

7. Acting on particular strategies to not only encourage buying customers to comment on their experience, verbally and online perhaps, but to come back and ideally tell all of their friends, when they have good things to say.

Every one of the above needs much planning and subsequent discussion to ensure that early efforts are smooth as the launch proceeds. Many startups (partly because of the early PR and marketing 'splash') can get good early results but as the impact of this fades and marketing spend is normalized it is then listening to customer feedback, pushing return visits, incenting people to bring others and other steps that will typically work best to drive sales upwards.

GRAND Step 2

Team resources and culture needed (internally/externally)

Once we have thought about the startup launch or re-launch planning, the growth path we think is attainable and the specific sustaining goals and timeline that makes most progressive sense, we can now start to consider how we best resource the forward plan, starting with the startup team.

We have already emphasized that the founder team should have direct internal skills and the early advisory or short-term consulting experience to be successful in the chosen beach-head target customer market during the SLAM process. However, the founder team now has to think about adding new people and ensuring they are able to make a major contribution to the growth goals and targets that are needed, including any new markets that it plans to attack. As we said earlier, these additional people should be able to work both hard and with much agility in often very fast-changing circumstances and ensure that they can stretch to higher goals of get the business from 'zero to 1'.

Clearly, this is more than simply adding people to loosely defined roles and hoping it works out. It actually means only adding people who can help the startup make a significant impact or get from zero to 1.

In this case, zero to 1 means the process of creating something radically new or different and taking it to a higher level than has been experienced before (or achieving major intensive growth) as opposed to creating only incremental improvements or moving at a slower pace to a product or service offering that only leads to a minor improvement over what was available before.

In practical terms, many successful and high growth startups talk about the need to hire 'A' players. These hires should typically want to stretch towards higher goals and make a difference with the product or service, or even make things transformationally different for the customer. To find these 'A' players (both on the team and as advisers) it's important to think about the key traits that you may want and need in your startup.

59

Although this may vary from one business to another, some traits that are often in the mix are an individual's capacity to be optimistic, take initiative, be enthusiastic, like to explore or be experimental, be organized, enlist cooperation from others, handle conflict well, be flexible, manage pressure well and be persistent (just to name a few).

It almost goes without saying that bringing on more staff to the startup will mean that effective leadership will become increasingly important, not just for the CEO, but also for the entire founder team.

In addition to hiring people who can help attain the goal of zero to 1 in the internal team, and making sure that people are well-led, it is also important for any startup to think about who can be of most assistance outside the business as a formal or informal adviser.

Informal advisers or consultants can be added for both short-term projects (and paid for short-term objectives or target completion) or as ongoing advisers or mentors, often paid on fixed retainer terms.

Sometimes these advisers can also be awarded shares options or small parcels of company stock to help lower short-term 'cash burn' or increase longer-term accountability and commitment. However, this is done, it is important to ensure that each adviser has relevant and explicitly needed knowledge and/or experience and that there is complete clarity about how the individual is intended to add value and assist in reaching ongoing growth goals.

Last, but not least, in this step, startup founders are always wise to give quality time to thinking carefully about the organizational culture and values that they would like to embed and to ensuring that these are adhered to as the company grows. This does not mean a quick brainstorming session on a few borrowed values from the walls of other startups and some general guidelines that have little or no tangible meaning. Instead, this should be a serious and careful debate about the way the founders would like to see things achieved by everyone and in what particular way. The clearer and better communicated this is for all to see and then borne out by founder actions, the better in the long-term – especially when new hires are recruited – and it might just head off all sorts of possible problems at a later stage!

For step 2, the key questions are:

Question 1: Which new people that should be progressively added directly to the team are best able to get from zero to 1 and help to reach our growth goals?

Question 2: Which external advisers, who should be progressively added directly to the team, are best able to help to reach our growth goals?

Question 3: What team and organizational culture and values should we craft and maintain to give the startup the best chance for long-term success?

GRAND Step 2

Team resources and evolving the culture

After a few months of running their first truck and starting to become more confident that the formula for success is now better understood, Hector and Maria think they are ready to buy a second food truck and hire people to operate it.

Before they place a job ad, Hector and Maria decide to make explicit all of the values that they have both personally and for the business and decide that apart from the 'green' and sustainability ones that are intrinsic to Fresh-Fare, there are others that are important too. These include outstanding service to customers, flexible teamwork, quality at all times and individual creativity. More personally they believe strongly in authenticity, humility, passion, and persistence. These are not only made into a little poster for each food truck but also added as a list to the service employee job description and used when writing the job advertisement.

Hector and Maria decide that they both individually need to develop their leadership skills and sign up for a leadership development program run out of a local college.

The two individuals hired have most of what Hector and Maria are looking for and have the added benefit of both being able to drive the food truck and do food preparation and service work. Both the man and woman they hire are very friendly and outgoing in personality and speak English and Spanish well. Although most food trucks pay minimum wage, Hector and Maria decided to give their new employees an extra dollar an hour and 0.5% of weekly revenues as a bonus.

On the adviser side, Maria concludes that Ron, the outside CPA, has a done a great job in helping Fresh-Fare to set up its chart of accounts online and showed them how to analyze their weekly sales figures by items sold, as well as how to use ratios to analyze overall business performance. He will now take a fee to help prepare their accounts at year-end and a bookkeeper will do an hour a day to keep the accounts in good order. Once again, Hector and Maria explain their values to the bookkeeper and treat the person as part of the team.

GRAND Step 3

Pricing and assumptions (including COCA AND LTV) to confirm long-term value and profitability

Because a startup will have established a reasonable level of market-product fit and thought about a 'first-cut' business and 'monetization' model that works for its initially targeted customers during the SLAM process, it should have already given some consideration to both how much value is added and what kind of pricing is likely to be acceptable.

Despite having a general idea from earlier work, on the GRAND side of the diagram, it is necessary to go much deeper into the value equation by getting considerably more explicit and being able to communicate this to customers so that they are willing to buy the product or service on offer. This essentially means that a startup should try as best it can to prove that it adds tangible value.

There are no explicit general guidelines on what 'value' means for customers, as it will depend on both the product/service and the particular customer group (and in some cases on the particular economic buyer identified). However, an example may help to illustrate how this may be done.

For instance, a medium-sized business may take an average of 15 days and eight people to close its accounting period books each quarter. With a new software product or platform supplied by a startup, this can mean the period to close the books can be reduced by 65% and the time of five people can be saved each quarter. This may mean a saving on the cost side of $100, 000 each year (saved employee time costs) and $80,00 on the revenue side (fast billing and more quickly received payments) making a total saving each year of $120,000 or $10,000 a month, on average.

If the SaaS fee for the software was $5,000 a month, this represents a net $5,000 saving to the company and a demonstrable value gain. This would clearly be very marginal if the SaaS fee per month was $10,000 or unattractive if the fee was more.

ıe-adding situations are as clear-cut as the accounting
ımple, but the effort to document this as best a the startup
l.

......g ıs often calculated in quite arbitrary ways by many startup
companies. This may be to merely 'plus up' from the cost of making
a product or the service, emulate a competitor price (undercutting it
a little perhaps) or even by making a crude estimate as to what the
target customer might be willing to bear. In addition, some startups
are often willing to discount their products or services in the short-
term to gain traction or even give them away for free, for a while at
least, which is rarely sustainable for very long. This is particularly
true for software-based products where the temptation to offer a free
version is high (to gain early users) in the hope that some of these
might be persuaded to upgrade to a paid version at a later stage. This
is much more difficult to do in practice than founders often think.

Perhaps the best way to go about pricing a product or service is to
know the overall unit economics of the particular startup business
and what it takes to supply the product or service (cover all costs,
including overheads) and to keep it less than the value that you are
adding for the customer (in both tangible and intangible ways).

In some cases, this will be simple (as the prior example shows) but
in other situations it might mean crafting some creative approaches,
(such as ramping up prices with the volume of users, for example, or
a fixed monthly or annual fee and 'use of product' charge, perhaps.
In all cases, the pricing model should always maintain the perception
(and reality of course) that considerable value is provided.

The last step, but perhaps most critical activity to be carried out
seriously in the GRAND process, is to calculate both the cost of
customer acquisition (COCA) and the long-term value (LTV) each
customer brings to the startup over time.

The COCA should be calculated on an overall basis (which is mainly
what marketing, sales, and related staffing costs are involved in
bringing each sale to the business). This is also usefully done later in
step 6 by each marketing channel, to make sure each one chosen is
cost effective.

shareholders on the sale of the company. Preferred stock also has the upside potential of being able to convert to common stock of the company. The majority of later financing rounds, after seed funding, are undertaken as convertible preferred stock. There is a strong benefit to the startup in issuing preferred stock to investors—it allows them to issue stock options (options to buy common stock, which does not enjoy preferred preferences) to prospective employees at a significantly reduced exercise price than that paid by the investors. This can provide a useful incentive to attract and retain the management team and employees.

Many experienced entrepreneurs and advisers will say that raising external capital is a dual-edged sword or cuts both ways.

On the one hand, assuming it is successful and the amount is appropriate to fund the plan, the startup now has more cash available to execute and deliver on its promises.

On the other hand, institutional investors will expect not only that the money is spent wisely but will want regular updates and reports (and may even have investors sit on the startup's board to ensure that this happens). This should present no real problem to a well-run startup but no founder team can predict the future and things will not always go to plan, and investors may look to make direct suggestions, sometimes aggressively so.

For instance, contracts can take longer to sign than expected, suppliers fail to deliver or have other problems, marketing spend may fail to attract prospects, sales may take longer to close than expected, customers may complain, etc. All of these examples, and many others mean that invested cash can be squeezed.

Although it does not diminish the chances of problems occurring, one way to make assure that the startup is better prepared for the roller-coaster ahead is to run sensitivity analysis. Sensitivity or scenario analysis aims to test the business model by considering changes of one or a combination of the variables defining the model. Such analysis helps to assess the weaknesses of the overall strategy, to assess the ability to pivot and even the ability to survive during the down market or fight competition when it drops prices.

For step 4, the key questions are:

Question 1: What capital do we need for the startup and at what point(s) will we need it, given our planned cash 'burn' rate and scaling plans?

Question 2: What form should the capital raise take and can it be phased?

Question 3: What sensitivity analysis should we have available to ensure that we can maximize our chances of using our invested capital wisely?

GRAND Step 4

Capital to be raised and phasing

Hector and Maria already had $150,000 in a bank savings account, mainly from Hector's early retirement package and paying off their home mortgage. They spent $50,000 on their first secondhand food truck and bought a second one in month 4 of their first year for the same price. With fitout and branding costs and initial supplies and inventory plus some costs for setting up their web site and mobile app, the couple has spent all of their savings and are now relying on their bank overdraft for credit. This gives them up to $10,000 if they need it.

When Hector and Maria analyze their business at the 6-month point, they see that monthly revenues are around $30,000 from both trucks, with around 2,100 covers supplied, out of which they are spending the following:

Labor	$7,500	Marketing	$5,000
Food supplies	$10,000	Phone/internet	$250
Consumables	$2,000	Licenses/permits	$750
Services/fees	$500	Insurance	$1,000
Fuel	$750	Miscellaneous	$1,250

This makes a total of $29,000 or a $1,000 gross profit. Maria suggests that one half of this is put away for future taxes so $500 a month can be saved for future investment and operational expansion (although the business is expected to grow by at least 25% on the same assets in the next two to three years). Because most of the costs are fixed (except labor, food supplies and consumables) gross revenues would grow to $37,500 a month and net of variable costs would thicken the overall profit amount to $3,500 per month (and net of tax cost savings, $2,500 of this would be available for future expansion).

To keep on growing, Hector and Maria decide that they could take out a loan of $50,000 from the bank and pay interest on it over 5 years, which would add $900 a month in debt fees and allow a third secondhand food truck to be acquired in the middle of their second year and have some additional cash on hand. Hector's parents are also willing to give the couple another $50,000 for a 1.5% equity stake, to which they agree.

GRAND Step 5

Capital deployment plans

While a calculation of the overall capital to be raised (and when) to fund the startup growth strategy is one part of the equation, the other side is the detailed planning that is always needed on how that money raised is to be deployed.

Once again, every startup will be different. For example, some are capital intensive and need to buy equipment or acquire supplies or product inventory, while others are not, such as app builders for instance. In the latter case, they may need to spend money on hiring staff aggressively, such as developers, in order to build software features and release upgrades and improvements quickly. But whatever the type of startup, there will be some common areas and investors will always want to see how much has been allocated to each category of intended spend.

One way to prepare to show how capital raised will be spent is to split costs into startup **expenses** and startup **assets** to be purchased.

Startup expenses can include costs such as legal work, website design or extensions, logo design, brochures, site location selection, and improvements. It also includes expenses such as rent and progressive payroll costs.

Typical startup assets are cash (in the form of the money in the bank when the company starts), and in some cases, starting supplies or inventory. Other starting assets might be current or long-term assets, such as equipment, office furniture and vehicles, for example.

The most important task in assembling this list of items on which money is intended to be spent in the future is to be prepared to answer the question, 'Why is this the case?' For example, 'Why commit to a three-year lease on an office or workspace when it could be for one year or a co-working space may be a better option?' The more that startup founders can ask themselves these type of questions, the better prepared they will be to answer such questions when put to them by investors.

The goal here, when developing a capital-spending plan, especially in a startup company environment, is always to conserve cash, especially in the period before fiscal breakeven. The more that the startup founders can demonstrate this kind of thinking, the better the investors usually like it, as it shows sound and prudent money management skills.

Once we have our long list of items on which we intend to spend capital, we should now review it, not only for its overall balance, timing, and effectiveness in achieving the growth goals of the startup but in ensuring that its main impact is on acquiring customers. Many startups, especially those that have been 'boot-strapping' for a long time, forget to do this and are too quick to move into a new office, buy new computers for everyone and even pay the founders more than the business can perhaps afford, in the short-term. While some of this may often be acceptable, it should not be at the expense of critical spending on customer acquisition and, in the final analysis, this means spending on marketing and sales.

Most institutional investors will expect a substantial proportion of a capital raise, especially at 'seed' and 'A round' equity level to be spent on marketing and sales, for the simple reason that it will drive revenue for the business and thereby reduce the rate at which capital raised is burned. As a rule of thumb, many investors will expect at least 50% of the raise to be spent on direct customer acquisition strategies and most will say it should be nearer to two thirds. This can and does vary for different types of startups (especially when they are heavily research-based or need to deal with considerable regulatory hurdles, for example). However, it is crucial to remember that practically all investors will take the view that customers 'pay the bills'; hence, acquiring them quickly and well is critical.

A final review at this step should be to make two broad estimates:

1. How long will the capital raised last, all things being equal, assuming that what has been forecast happens pretty much to plan? This might be nine months, a year or even 18 months, or what is often called the 'runway' period.

2. When might we need to raise capital again to grow further and if we do, how much should we be thinking about raising at that time?

This second question is more difficult because startup founders have to guess about what might go well or wrong and allow for a period when the founders are pitching for capital but not obtaining it. Either way, investors will often expect a 'best estimate' and expect the founders to be able to explain their logic.

For step 5, the key questions are:

Question 1: In what specific areas will capital be spent and why?

Question 2: In what specific and substantial ways will we be deploying capital (and how much of it) to acquire customers versus everything else?

Question 3: How much estimated 'runway' will this capital give us, and when are we likely to need to raise capital again and how much (if we do)?

GRAND Step 5

Capital deployment planning

Having raised $100,000 in additional expansion capital, $50,000 in a loan from the bank and $50,000 as an equity stake in the business, Hector and Maria are very open to showing both of their investors that they have a good forward plan.

In year 2 of the business, they will buy a third food truck at $50,000, and then the plan is to do the same in years 3, 4 and 5 until they have six total paid for out of future revenues.

Given that they expect to spend 60% of their current investment of $100,000 on their new truck purchase and fitout (leaving only $40,000), Hector and Maria know that they will need to spend another $180,000 to buy their last 3 food trucks and fit them out (or a net capital need of $140,000) assuming no other unforeseen problems come up and the business expands as expected.

Hector and Maria worked with Ron their CPA to offer the analysis on the following page.

	Sales Year 1	Sales Year 2	Sales Year 3	Sales Year 4	Sales Year 5	Sales Year 6
Food Truck 1 (Year 0)	$250,000	$300,000	$375,000	$375,000	$375,000	$375,000
Food Truck 2 (Year 1)	$150,000	$300,000	$375,000	$375,000	$375,000	$375,000
Food Truck 3 (Year 2)	$0	$150,000	$300,000	$375,000	$375,000	$375,000
Food Truck 4 (Year 3)	$0	$0	$150,000	$300,000	$375,000	$375,000
Food Truck 5 (Year 4)	$0	$0	$0	$150,000	$300,000	$375,000
Food Truck 6 (Year 5)	$0	$0	$0	$0	$150,000	$300,000
Total revenues	**$400,000**	**$750,000**	**$1,200,000**	**$1,575,000**	**$1,950,000**	**$2,175,000**
Costs – fixed	48,000	75,000	110,000	150,000	185,000	215,000
Costs – variable	$260,000	$487,500	$780,000	$1,023,750	$1,267,500	$1,413,750
Costs – total	**$308,000**	**$562,500**	**$890,000**	**$1,173,750**	**$1,452,500**	**$1,628,750**
Gross margin	**$92,000**	**$187,500**	**$310,000**	**$401,250**	**$497,500**	**$546,250**
Gross margin %	23.0%	25.0%	25.8%	25.5%	25.5%	25.1%
Available for growth	**$59,800**	**$121,875**	**$201,500**	**$260,813**	**$323,375**	**$355,063**

GRAND Step 6

Organizational systems design and support resources needed

In the very early stages, a startup has almost no organization. It's all hands on deck and founders have no choice but to wear many 'hats' and get things done given that things often go forward, backward and sideways frequently.

In practice, this kind of loose organizational structure and just-in-time resource provision may go on for a very long time – months or even years! But after the validation phase is over and especially when outside capital is brought in, not only do investors want to see more organization, structure, and systems in the startup, but the founders may be grateful for greater predictability and certainty.

The level or amount of organizational systems and support resources to be introduced will very much depend on the startup and its focus and type. However, let's look at these broad areas where some organization is expected.

(a) Organizational design and management structure

As a startup matures, it is natural for teams to form. These might be teams such as development, operations, sales, marketing, product, technology, customer service, administration, and even founder/executive.

When there were only a few people wearing multiple hats structure probably didn't matter. However, as the company grows, structure becomes important to decision-making and overall efficiency and the founders or executives should start to focus on working more *on* the business rather than *in* the business.

For the most part, this means establishing clear reporting lines and responsibilities and even task lists or job descriptions, coupled with OKRs developed for the venture at an overall level at the SLAM stage for all departments and even all individuals.

(b) Human resources (HR) processes

Few very early stage startups need to think much about HR, but when a business has more than 12 to 15 employees, some thought as to organization in this area can pay huge long-term dividends.

HR is a broad discipline but within it hiring looms as the one area where good systems and support can be extremely helpful. This includes using outside agencies or resources to guide founders to applicant tracking systems, candidate profiling tools, interviewee screening systems, and even background and reference checking services to ensure that candidates for positions are identified and selected in the most optimal ways possible.

HR is also an area where structured and defensible compensation planning can be worthwhile. This should start with robust founder agreements about pay and equity positions, but extends to other employee salaries and benefits, to help attract people and systems for paying benefits, including commissions and bonuses, and even awarding stock options.

A third realm for HR systems is in the area of EEO and diversity. Although there are some legal requirements to be met here, especially ensuring that there is a policy against unfair discrimination or workplace harassment, it's critical to build a fair and consistent culture in which there is equal opportunity for career advancement and that there is as much diversity on the team as possible.

In this last area, this does not just mean gender, age or racial diversity, but also diversity in thinking and approach. It is well documented that some of the most successful and innovative startups in the past have had what many experts see as a highly positive culture and a big part of this is seen to be having the most diverse people on the team from the very earliest stages.

(c) Regulatory issues

Finally in this step, regulatory issues may increasingly arise as being in need of attention as the team grows, and help from professionals such as attorneys, accountants, and others is well worth having close at hand.

Although this will often depend mostly on the industry or sector and location in which the startup operates, primary areas for regulatory focus are in the realms of intellectual property or IP protection (to ensure that the startup owns its assets and those that employees may come up with while working for it), taxation issues (where a little forward planning can save considerable money down the track) and other legal issues. The last of these is obviously something of a catch-all but will often include sound company formation documents, well-written contracts and agreements, well-written stock issuing certificates, good business terms and conditions statements and robust confidentiality agreements, just to name a few.

For step 6, the key questions are:

Question 1: What organizational design and management structure will serve us best over the short- to medium-term?

Question 2: What are our best short-term HR processes (including hiring, compensation, EEO, diversity, etc.) going forward?

Question 3: To what regulatory issues do we need to pay the most attention in the short- to medium-term and why (IP, Legal, Taxation, etc.)?

GRAND Step 6

Organization systems design

Hector and Maria are second-generation Hispanics and speak both English and Spanish and well understand both cultures. Their children, who work part-time and occasionally for the business, are obviously third-generation but only speak limited Spanish. Hector and Maria are very focused on recruiting diverse people as new food trucks are bought and this includes diversity of age, gender, ethnicity but also covering people with very different personalities even though they all have a common interest in 'green' and sustainable approaches.

During the first year, Hector and Maria made most of these business decisions, with the occasional help of advisers Ron and Paula. However, by the second year, they decided that better organization and structure was necessary. As a result, they decide to assign all food truck scheduling, operations and food and consumable supply to Hector and assign everything else, including all administrative, budgeting, cost control, accounting and HR to Maria. They also assigned the external advisers to Maria to talk with and then institute a monthly web conference meeting for all staff at 8.30 am on a Saturday morning for 60 minutes to discuss any problems and share comments and ideas across the business. This included discussing new possible candidates to join Fresh-Fare as the business expands, as they are put forward by the external recruitment agency, the manager of which is also on the call.

Hector and Maria use their monthly meeting to discuss business performance and talk about their 5 key OKRs around numbers of customers served, covers per day, revenue per week, supply chain efficiency and customer satisfaction and referrals. This includes compensation and benefits openly and how much is available in the bonus pool each month for distribution.

Fresh-Fare is always looking to ensure that it is operating fairly and within the law and asks all of its employees to ensure that all licenses and other regulations are adhered to in every location in which a food truck operates. This means that everyone is vigilant about regulations and changes that must be addressed.

GRAND Step 7

Infrastructure needs and 'make or buy' decisions

Particularly when a startup has raised money and begins to spend it, the company will start to feel increasingly like a real business with a group of people coming together to achieve a number of goals in a variety of collective ways. But at the same time, what the startup could achieve day-by-day with the founders and a few people early on, and with little outside help, begins to shift and new decisions have to be made about how things get done.

The three biggest changes in this regard are:

1. What should, or even must, we do ourselves?

2. What can we get done by others outside the business?

3. How can we stay innovative or be creative around our tasks and processes to get work done efficiently and effectively?

Deciding what to keep in-house is a discussion to be had within the founder team and other executives/external advisers so that this team can decide the 'why' or the key reasons that a particular function is core to the startup's DNA.

It can, but doesn't always have to, be areas such as development or design work, marketing, sales, and customer service. However, even these functions can often be performed well by outside firms, at least for a while, to help save cash or reduce overhead and commitments, or reduce risk.

Once we have a good idea about what we must keep in-house, we can now evaluate what work has the potential to be done by outsiders (outsourced locally or even done outside the state or country, where this makes sense).

In a hardware startup, for example, it is possible to manufacturer very cost-effectively in countries such as China, Mexico or South Korea, or, in a software startup, to have some development work done quickly and at a much lower hourly rate in countries such as India or a country in Eastern Europe, perhaps. This helps to not only keep overhead costs lower in the short-term but, perhaps, get a product shipped more quickly.

Care needs to be taken to think about management and coordination, not to mention IP protection, when making such decisions about how work gets done but these can often be overcome with a little planning and good organization at the outset.

Finally, at this step, we need to keep an eye on how the startup progresses and grows as things can change quickly. Processes that we thought were better done in-house (like marketing, for instance) could be done by bigger agencies that well understand the sector a startup might be focused upon, as they may have a much wider reach.

Other functions, that looked much cheaper to 'buy in' as a service or to outsource, may become difficult to manage or have unexpected quality problems or irritating shipping delays. In these circumstances, it becomes more effective to bring the tasks back in-house and hire people directly, over which the startup will then have greater control.

Naturally, there is no set formula for 'make or buy' and this changes all the time as a startup gathers experience in its market. The point here is that founders need to be agile and constantly on the lookout to be creative in how to get from A to B – as the saying goes, 'There are many ways to skin a cat.'

For step 7, the key questions are:

Question 1: What tasks or which processes do we absolutely want/need to keep in-house or do ourselves and why?

Question 2: What tasks or which processes can we outsource/offshore or buy in to help keep our fixed infrastructure and overhead costs as low as possible?

Question 3: What creative approaches can we take to getting startup work or tasks done and, in so doing, to conserve our cash?

GRAND Step 7

Infrastructure needs

Hector and Maria quickly realize that in all of the many factors that they have to manage to help make the business a success and a profitable one, the time taken to serve customers is probably the most crucial one. It means not only that customers get their food or drinks quicker, which they like of course, but also that the preparation time can be made much shorter and potentially easier for the staff.

In the first few months, Hector and Maria made every order from scratch to deliver on their promise of freshness. However, this made some tasks very slow. The two slowest were the fruit and vegetable juices and salads.

For the juices, Hector and Maria wanted to maintain daily freshness and assemble the choices people make as they are ordered. However, they can buy their fruit and vegetables on a daily basis, which are pre-peeled and often cut up. They can also make their pre-squeezed lemon juice the evening before and at the same time grill the proteins for tomorrow's salads. Continuing with the salad side of things, each food truck team can buy their four green-leaf ingredients (butter-lettuce, arugula, spinach, and romaine) pre 'torn up' and have some of their additional items supplied in bulk (walnuts, almonds, cheese, etc.) to add. As we said earlier, salad dressings (of various interesting kinds) will be supplied in attractive little jars for each individual to add on their own (and then return for 50 cents back).

The other big area in which Fresh-Fare needs help is marketing. Although some skills exist internally, this needs both professional experts and a relentless focus on a day-by-day basis. This includes testing different advertisement types and channels and making sure that daily social media communications go out on a regular basis and in an accurate way.

Hector and Maria (with Paula's help to set it up well) find a marketing support company in Arizona that will do this for a fixed fee each month. They also hire a 'virtual assistant' in India to help them coordinate all of their social media activities and even respond to customer feedback online.

GRAND Step 8

Start-up fiscal projections: (a) Major confirmed business and fiscal assumptions, (b) P&L, (c) 5-year cash-flow, (d) 5-year budget

In this final step of the GRAND process (and it's a big, multi-part step), founders need to have highly robust fiscal projections for the startup, which will become critical measures of commercial success going forward. Although this essentially involves a well-crafted three to five-year projected profit and loss statement, cash-flow statement, balance sheet and budget, the journey to creating these should ideally commence with two activities:

1. Listing all the assumptions upon which the fiscal projections will rest and/or depend; and

2. Understanding where assumption sensitivity analysis needs to be performed.

Fiscal assumptions are relatively straightforward to list. The cost of production, cost of labor, number of customers, number of sales at a given price (and the velocity with which they occur) and even the weekly or monthly costs of marketing and sales can all underpin the numbers on a financial spreadsheet. This may vary from one startup to the next depending upon where it is focused. However, the major assumptions are likely to be relatively common ones, leaving a few additional ones that are specific to the particular startup.

Assumptions always need considerable discussion and agreement within the team to make sure they are realistic and that they are detailed enough to make a constructed spreadsheet reflect what is likely to happen, at least as closely as possible, including what a possible exit strategy might be for the business at some point in the future.

Sensitivity analysis is a little more complicated because, in theory, every assumption can be analyzed and multiple scenarios, both positive and negative, calculated. However, the most common assumptions to which sensitivity analysis is most often applied are the number of customers, the velocity and cost of their acquisition (including customer 'churn'), price, and sometimes overall revenue. In addition, on the cost side, manufacturing and/or production and delivery costs are often also included.

In combination, the assumptions made, and the sensitivity analysis that applies to some of them, are often called the fundamental 'unit economics' of the business and are regularly called for as an early summary of overall performance by institutional investors, for example, so that they can get a quick snapshot of how reasonable the numbers appear to be, at first look.

For step 8 the key questions are:

Question 1: On what key assumptions do our fiscal projections for the next three to five years rest and why?

Question 2: In what areas should we have available sensitivity analysis on our fiscal projections and why?

Question 3: What do our prospective P&L, balance sheet, cash-flow, and budget documents tell us about how we should best manage our business going forward?

GRAND Step 8

Fiscal projections

Fresh-Fare's assumptions (especially as they mainly relate to unit economic are concerned) are as follows:

1. A food truck can serve 150 covers a day, 5 days a week and another 50 on a weekend day.

2. A food truck can operate for 300 days of the year on a minimum basis.

3. An average cover (per customer) will be $10 to $11.

4. A food truck (based on the above can make $375,000 on weekdays and another $25,000 on weekends.

5. This can be earned by having 2 opening hours each day of 5 hours maximum.

6. The addressable college market in Orange County is over 300,000 people.

7. The average cost of food and drink ingredients will be 40% of revenues.

8. The average cost of labor will be 25% of revenues.

9. The average customer (18 to 22 years of age) has $100 to spend on eating out each week (on food and drink).

10. The cost of customer acquisition will be $2.78 or less.

Clearly, all of the above unit economics can be open to sensitivity analysis and it is always wise for a startup to perform this analysis by individual item and in a combination of several factors. Unit economics, like price, is relatively linear but in this case, it could be useful to move away from an average cover number and get into drinks versus food and even split up food items.

Other factors might be more pivotal to success for Fresh-Fare. For example, covers per weekday need to have sensitivities of perhaps 5%, 10% and even 20% up and down around this assumption and even look to see where minimum covers are necessary to reach break-even for a given day.

Another factor to consider is analyzing labor costs. In a business like this labor is not a variable but a fixed cost. Fresh-Fare can, therefore, handle more volume than forecast without adding extra staff and perhaps use staff to help in different ways.

Once assumptions have been listed and sensitivity analysis performed (and changes made where this is suggested by the data, of course) we can now prepare each of the four fiscal projections that should be created (or at least we can hire a financial expert and guide him or her to do it for us). The first of these is usually the prospective or proforma profit and loss statement

(a) The profit and loss statement (P&L)

When a startup is new or at the earliest stages of its life, it rarely has the information to prepare a real or actual P&L statement, so best guesses and estimates have to be made. A proforma statement is usually prepared for each month of the first year in business, and then more months are added for at least 3 or, more often, 5 years to the projection to show when the profit occurs and when the business is generating positive cash-flow on a consistent basis (and an 'earnings before interest, tax, depreciation, amortization' or EBITDA can be calculated). In simple terms, a P&L is built as follows:

1. Estimate sales and resultant revenues for each month. Ideally, revenues are best under-estimated, both in timing and amount.

2. Estimate cost of sales (often called cost of goods sold or COGS). These are often variable with the volume of goods or services sold. For example, in a manufacturing business, raw materials or semi-finished goods might be a COGS line item.

3. All possible expenses startup founders think should be in the statement are listed including all labor, sales and marketing costs, rent, lease costs, insurance, legal costs, etc. In this case, these line items should be over-estimated so those founders aren't later surprised. Don't forget, it's also important to also add a category and amount for miscellaneous items for the often many expenses founders may forget to include.

4. The difference between sales/revenues and COGs plus expenses is usually negative for some period of time, which is why startups often seek grants, borrow money or seek equity.

Fresh-Fare's proforma profit and loss or income statement as they finish the SLAM diagram is shown on the next page.

SLAM Case Study: Fresh-Fare Food Trucks

Income Statement	Projected				
	Year 1	Year 2	Year 3	Year 4	Year 5
Sales (Income)	$800,000	$1,200,000	$1,600,000	$2,000,000	$2,400,000
Cost of Sales (COGS)					
Food Purchases	$320,000	$480,000	$640,000	$800,000	$960,000
Direct Labor	156,000	245,700	386,978	496,621	663,666
Cost of Sales (COGS)	$476,000	$725,700	$1,026,978	$1,296,621	$1,623,666
Gross Profit	$324,000	$474,300	$573,022	$703,379	$776,334
Gross Profit Margin	40.50%	39.53%	35.81%	35.17%	32.35%
S,G, & A Expenses					
Marketing	80,000	120,000	160,000	200,000	240,000
Operational Costs	80,000	90,000	80,000	100,000	120,000
Occupancy	–	5,000	5,000	5,000	5,000
Insurance	10,000	10,000	10,000	10,000	10,000
Legal	10,000	5,000	5,000	5,000	5,000
Accounting	5,000	7,500	7,500	7,500	7,500
Owner Compensation	–	25,000	50,000	75,000	100,000
Other	24,000	36,000	48,000	60,000	72,000
S,G, & A Expenses	$209,000	$298,500	$365,500	$462,500	$559,500
EBITDA	$115,000	$175,800	$207,522	$240,879	$216,834
Depreciation	–	–	–	–	–
Pre Tax Profit	$115,000	$175,800	$207,522	$240,879	$216,834

(b) The cash-flow statement

Most simply, cash-flow statements quickly tell the story of how much revenue a company has coming in (inflows), and how much revenue it has going out (outflows) in real time. That information can be leveraged to gauge a startup's progressive liquidity and to predict where it will stand financially in the near future.

The cash-flow statement typically records the inflow and outflow of cash between the external world and the startup during a particular period, such as quarter-by-quarter and then year-by-year, although many investors like to see that startup founders have a month-by-month version of this.

The cash-flow statement provides the link that connects the income statement to the balance sheet and aids in understanding how one affects the other. It shows the impact of the revenue and profit-generating activities – usually referred to as operating activities – on the company's cash. It also records the impact of investing, which includes asset purchases and sales, and financing, which includes debt financing and equity contributions and withdrawals, on the company's cash.

For founders, the cash-flow statement is the one to watch the most closely month to month. This is because it so readily shows 'cash-burn', looming funding gaps and when break-even or profitability points will theoretically be reached.

Cash is king in a startup business and a well built cash-flow statement, that is regularly updated, will help that startup to survive the 'valley of death' (or the period when revenues are smaller than all business expenses!).

Fresh-Fare's proforma cash-flow statement as they finish the SLAM diagram is shown on the next page.

SLAM Case Study: Fresh-Fare Food Trucks

Cash-Flow Statement	Projected				
	Year 1	Year 2	Year 3	Year 4	Year 5
Cash-Flow from Operations					
Sales (Income)	$800,000	$1,200,000	$1,600,000	$2,000,000	$2,400,000
Cost of Sales (COGS)	$476,000	$725,700	$1,026,978	$1,296,621	$1,623,666
Gross Profit	**$324,000**	**$474,300**	**$573,022**	**$703,379**	**$776,334**
S,G, & A Expenses	$233,000	$334,500	$413,500	$522,500	$631,500
Operating Profit	**$91,000**	**$139,800**	**$159,522**	**$180,879**	**$144,834**
Interest Expense	–	–	–	–	–
Net Profit Before Taxes	**$91,000**	**$139,800**	**$159,522**	**$180,879**	**$144,834**
Taxes Paid	–	–	–	–	–
Net Income	**$91,000**	**$139,800**	**$159,522**	**$180,879**	**$144,834**
Add Back Depreciation	$24,000	$36,000	$48,000	$60,000	$72,000
Dec (Inc) in Accounts Receivable	–	–	–	–	–
Dec (Inc) in Inventory	–	–	–	–	–
Dec (Inc) in Other Current Assets	–	–	–	–	–
Inc (Dec) in Accounts Payable	–	–	–	–	–
Inc (Dec) in Other Current Liabilities	–	–	–	–	–
Cash-Flow from Operations	**$115,000**	**$175,800**	**$207,522**	**$240,879**	**$216,834**
Cash-Flow from Investments					
Capital Expenditures	($120,000)	($60,000)	($60,000)	($60,000)	($60,000)
Dec (Inc) in Other Assets	–	–	–	–	–
Cash-Flow from Investments	**($120,000)**	**($60,000)**	**($60,000)**	**($60,000)**	**($60,000)**
Cash-Flow from Financing Activities					
Inc (Dec) in Short-Term Debt	–	–	–	–	–
Inc (Dec) in Loan from Owners	–	–	–	–	–
Inc (Dec) in Other Long-Term Liabilities	–	–	–	–	–
Inc (Dec) in Preferred Stock	–	–	–	–	–
Inc (Dec) in Common Stock	$130,000	–	–	–	–
Inc (Dec) in Add Paid-in Capital	–	–	–	–	–
Dividends Paid/Withdrawals	–	–	–	–	–
Cash-Flow from Financing Activities	**$130,000**	–	–	–	–
Net Free Cash-Flow	**$125,000**	**$115,800**	**$147,522**	**$180,879**	**$156,834**
Beginning Total Cash	–	**$125,000**	**$240,800**	**$388,322**	**$569,201**
Ending Total Cash	**$125,000**	**$240,800**	**$388,322**	**$569,201**	**$726,035**

(c) The balance sheet

A balance sheet is a business statement that shows what the startup owns, what it owes, and the value of the owner's investment in the business. The balance sheet is calculated at a specific point in time – at business startup; and prospectively at the end of a month, a quarter, or a year; or eventually at the end of the business or when it gets sold.

A balance sheet is always prepared by using two columns, typically with assets on the left and liabilities and owner's equity on the right. The total assets must equal total liabilities + total owners equity; that is, the two totals must balance.

Steps in preparing a business startup balance sheet are as follows:

1. First, list the value of all the assets in the business either as the startup commences or when it is launched in earnest. This includes cash, equipment, and vehicles, supplies, inventory, prepaid items (insurance, for example), and the value of any buildings or land owned if this applies.

2. Sometimes, accounts receivable are included as an asset, but since the business has not started, there is rarely any money owed to the business unless early products have been shipped on consignment perhaps and there are expectations for any items sold are paid for.

3. Next, all current and prospective liabilities are listed (amounts owed by the business to others), including business credit cards, any loans to the business at startup, and any amounts owed to vendors at startup. Add up the total liabilities.

4. The difference between assets and liabilities is shown on the right side of the balance sheet as 'Owner's Equity' (for an unincorporated business) or 'Retained Earnings' (for a corporation). This amount is the startup founder's investment in the business.

One final note is important here. Although it's not directly part of the balance sheet at a detailed level, the other document that most investors will want to see in a startup business is the 'cap' or capitalization table.

A cap table provides a clear analysis of the startup's percentages of ownership, equity dilution, and value of equity in each round of investment by founders, investors, and other owners (even early and tiny ones).

Fresh-Fare's proforma balance sheet as they finish the SLAM diagram is shown on the next page.

SLAM Case Study: Fresh-Fare Food Trucks

Balance Sheet	Projected				
	Year 1	Year 2	Year 3	Year 4	Year 5
Cash (Bank Funds)	$125,000	$240,800	$388,322	$569,201	$726,035
Accounts Receivable	–	–	–	–	–
Inventory	–	–	–	–	–
Other Current Assets	–	–	–	–	–
Total Current Assets	**$125,000**	**$240,800**	**$388,322**	**$569,201**	**$726,035**
Gross Fixed Assets	$120,000	$180,000	$240,000	$300,000	$360,000
Accumulated Depreciation	($24,000)	($60,000)	($108,000)	($168,000)	($240,000)
Net Fixed Assets	**$96,000**	**$120,000**	**$132,000**	**$132,000**	**$120,000**
Other Assets	–	–	–	–	–
Total Assets	**$221,000**	**$360,800**	**$520,322**	**$701,201**	**$846,035**
Accounts Payable	–	–	–	–	–
Short-Term Debt	–	–	–	–	–
Other Current Liabilities	–	–	–	–	–
Total Current Liabilities	–	–	–	–	–
Loan from Owners	–	–	–	–	–
Other Long-Term Liabilities	–	–	–	–	–
Total Long-Term Liabilities	–	–	–	–	–
Total Liabilities	–	–	–	–	–
Preferred Stock	–	–	–	–	–
Common Stock	$130,000	$130,000	$130,000	$130,000	$130,000
Additional Paid-in Capital	–	–	–	–	–
Dividends Paid/Withdrawals	–	–	–	–	–
Ending Retained Earnings	$91,000	$230,800	$390,322	$571,201	$716,035
Total Equity	**$221,000**	**$360,800**	**$520,322**	**$701,201**	**$846,035**
Total Liabilities + Equity	**$221,000**	**$360,800**	**$520,322**	**$701,201**	**$846,035**

(d) The startup budget

A startup budget is like a projected cash-flow statement, but with a little more guesswork. It is subsequently used to compare budgeted line items and actual expenditures or what is often called variance analysis. Startups should build a budget even if it doesn't need funds from investors.

In basic terms, a budget shows what you expect to bring in and how much to expect to spend each month, by detailed line item. This is not only good for startup founders and senior executives to use but institutional investors will also want to know that startup leaders can follow a budget and not overspend without good reasons to do so (and use variance analysis to alert investors to possible future cash problems).

Investors are also likely to want to see how much founders are likely to need to pay bills on a month-by-month basis while the business is starting out (working capital), and how long it will take the startup to have a positive cash-flow (bring in more money than is being spent).

Like the other financial statements, a typical budget should be carried through five years, but in this particular case 3 and even 2 years is often deemed to be sufficient.

A budget can also be prepared for physical assets, including items such as depreciation that might apply (hence the example on the next page).

Fresh-Fare's proforma food truck budget and depreciation schedule as they finish the SLAM diagram is shown on the next page.

SLAM Case Study: Fresh-Fare Food Trucks

Capex	Projected				
	Year 1	Year 2	Year 3	Year 4	Year 5
Purchase Cost	$120,000	$60,000	$60,000	$60,000	$60,000
Depreciation	($24,000)	($36,000)	($48,000)	($60,000)	($72,000)
NET Carrying Value	**$96,000**	**$120,000**	**$132,000**	**$132,000**	**$120,000**
# Trucks Purchased	2	1	1	1	1
TOTAL # Trucks	**2**	**3**	**4**	**5**	**6**

Depreciation Policy
Straight Line Depreciation

5	Useful life (years)
$60,000	Cost for a used Food Truck [includes assumption of $15,000 for retrofitting]

Vehicle # 1					
Purchase Cost	$60,000	–	–	–	–
Depreciation	($12,000)	($12,000)	($12,000)	($12,000)	($12,000)
NET Carrying Value	**$48,000**	**$36,000**	**$24,000**	**$12,000**	**–**
Vehicle # 2					
Purchase Cost	$60,000	–	–	–	–
Depreciation	($12,000)	($12,000)	($12,000)	($12,000)	($12,000)
NET Carrying Value	**$48,000**	**$36,000**	**$24,000**	**$12,000**	**–**
Vehicle # 3					
Purchase Cost	–	$60,000	–	–	–
Depreciation	–	($12,000)	($12,000)	($12,000)	($12,000)
NET Carrying Value	**–**	**$48,000**	**$36,000**	**$24,000**	**$12,000**
Vehicle # 4					
Purchase Cost	–	–	$60,000	–	–
Depreciation	–	–	($12,000)	($12,000)	($12,000)
NET Carrying Value	**–**	**–**	**$48,000**	**$36,000**	**$24,000**
Vehicle # 5					
Purchase Cost	–	–	–	$60,000	–
Depreciation	–	–	–	($12,000)	($12,000)
NET Carrying Value	**–**	**–**	**–**	**$48,000**	**$36,000**
Vehicle # 6					
Purchase Cost	–	–	–	–	$60,000
Depreciation	–	–	–	–	($12,000)
NET Carrying Value	**–**	**–**	**–**	**–**	**$48,000**

Fresh-Fare after the GRAND diagram is completed

This is an invented case study, so any wrap-up summary is at best a guess, based on the customer discovery and data gathered. However, this case study is based on a real food truck startup so let's summarize what is likely to be the current focus and future prospects for Hector and Maria and Fresh-Fare.

As we can see throughout the case study, Hector and Maria carefully did the analysis they needed to do at each stage to make sure that they not only validated their assumptions, hypotheses, and guesses about this business, and what the customer might like and want, but also developed specific strategies and tactics to meet customer needs once they became known.

As we suggested earlier, this is a time for clear-eyed thinking and not blind optimism so it is equally important to find out that assumptions are wrong as to find out you are right (and sometimes it's a little of each).

Because the GRAND diagram is an execution-centered template and mainly about making sure that this business can be profitable (both for Hector and Maria and for investors) the financial projections that are shown are clearly extremely positive. If these were real Hector and Maria would be wise to double check that they have not missed anything important and perhaps engaged in a little pessimistic or 'black-hat analysis' to assess what could go wrong in the future or dent business performance significantly.

GRAND summary

The GRAND process is intended to be a simple template to help founders who have validated their startup to execute efficiently and effectively their plans for growth and establishing customer traction. This means thinking through, organizing and resourcing a range of actions that will need to be taken to ensure that sound progress is made on multiple fronts.

As startup founders (and others they have hired) have progressed on their journey, by using the GRAND process, they will have gathered information on all eight steps below:

1. Detailed startup launch, growth path and sustaining goals/ timeline.

2. Team resources and culture needed (internally/externally).

3. Pricing and assumptions (including COCA and LTV) to confirm long-term value and profitability.

4. Capital raise and phasing needs.

5. Capital deployment plans.

6. Organizational systems design and support resources needed.

7. Infrastructure needs and 'make or buy' decisions.

8. Fiscal projections including (a) Major confirmed business and fiscal assumptions, (b) 5-year revenue projections, COGS, expenses, profit and EBITDA, (c) 5-year cash-flow including breakeven and (d) 5-year projected budget including fixed and variable.

In essence, the eight steps are a process for ensuring a high level of focus, commitment, and accountability at all levels.

An example of what the Fresh-Fare GRAND one page diagram could look like is shown on the next page.

The areas of focus, commitment, and accountability mentioned above has three main questions that should be asked:

Question 1: On what should we focus most and when (and does everyone on the team know this, especially when circumstances change)?

Question 2: Are specific individuals committed to objectives and key results?

Question 3: Is each person on the management team clearly and tangibly accountable for particular startup growth/business outcomes, including financial ones?

We hope this process helps with these questions.

GRAND for Fresh-Fare

1

Focus on early student customers (mainly college students in OC):
- Bought 1st truck and testing college campus with lunch and dinner traffic and sales
- Carefully tabulate customer frequency and type
- Buy 2nd truck and prepare big PR launch of business with mailing and media
- Launch app and carry out PR campaign and big push on social media
- Set up simply daily and weekly account system

4

Capital rise and phasing:
- All marketing at 25% of revenues means a $2.78 per customer cost of acquisition
- Repeat customers in the 1st year were around 50% and steadily growing
- Can use reserves and revenue but may need $50K to $100K

5

Capital deployment plans:
- Raise $50K on debt financing (bank loan adds $900 a month to expenses)
- Raise $50K in equity financing – offer 1.5% of business as equity plus return original investment over 5 years from year 2

3

Pricing and assumptions:
- Use new capital to buy second and third food truck
- Use profits from normal operations to complete design and fit-outs on both new trucks
- Trucks 4, 5 and 6 including necessary fit-outs should be possible out of future business cash-flows
- Price target at $9 min per cover (maximize $1 tip potential)
- Plan on retaining customers for 3 years
- At 10 purchases per year LTV is $270 per customer

8

- P&L summary data including profit and EBITDA
- Proforma data

2

Add full-time marketing resource – culture of friendly service

6

Resources needed:
- Assign food truck scheduling, operations, food and consumable supply to Hector
- Assign everything else, including admin, budgeting, cost control, accounting and HR to Maria
- Institute a monthly web conference meeting for all staff

5 year cash flow:
- Month by month
- By food truck
- Net cash

5 year projected budget:
- Summary budget data
- 'Float' needs

What we believe:
- College students want 'green' food from mobile trucks and are willing to pay $10 for the privilege

7

Infrastructure:
- Investigate buying pre-peeled and cut fruit and veg on daily basis
- Pre-squeeze lemon juice and grill proteins for salads the evening before
- Find marketing supply company to help with daily social media postings

Assumptions: College students are willing to spend $10 each time they visit a food truck. Each truck will 150 covers a day.

98

Case study summary

As Fresh-Fare is a fictitious case study, in some respects we cannot say how successful Hector and Maria's business could or would be, if it were real. However, we can suggest two ways to look at it:

- Highly optimistically, where all the SLAM diagram hypotheses and assumptions are proved and subsequent execution and results are even better than was expected by the business founders.

- Highly pessimistically, when many of the SLAM diagram hypotheses and assumptions are not proved and subsequent execution and results are far inferior to what was expected by the business founders.

Let's look at an optimistic scenario for this business first:

- Fresh-Fare could have tapped into a major food trend by offering 'green and healthy' products from their food truck. This could be more popular with the Millennials and Gen Z in particular, so in practice, this may widen the customer base from 15 to 40 years of age and drive many more customers to their food trucks than they forecast.

- Customers may refer many friends both verbally and via their smartphones, as well as through social media, thereby increasing numbers of customers, especially as they increase targeted marketing spend.

- Fresh-Fare's menu choices could have proved not only popular but easy and quick to prepare and serve – each customer could be served in 60 seconds on average – crucial when serving at busy times (making cover sales greater).

- Some food items may prove super popular (like the eggs or the fruit/veg juices) and bring in much more revenue than forecast.

- They could have easily added items for high margin profit like organic tea and coffee for example.

- Some items like salads with interesting or very different dressings may provide opportunities to add new revenue lines like selling dressing in jars separately.

- Having six food trucks are likely to provide food and consumable item purchasing economies of scale over competitors with just one or two food trucks.

- There are more windows for Fresh-Fare to open or be available – at breakfast or more on weekends for example – making asset utilization higher.

- Fresh-Fare has many opportunities in markets/gatherings outside college campuses, such as local weddings, galas, fêtes, exhibitions, conferences, etc.

- Customers could be willing to pay more for the quality on offer.

Now let's look at the other side of the coin and a pessimistic scenario for this business:

- There may be too few people close by at meal times, leaving many waiting periods with no or few customers.

- Food may not be served fast enough when lines are long and people leave to eat/drink elsewhere.

- Prices may be perceived to be too high compared to other alternatives (especially fast food or on-campus venue choices) that may be closely available.

- As much as people say they want fresh and healthy food, other less healthy options are often tempting, not to mention sometimes cheaper and easy to access, taking business away from Fresh-Fare.

- Other competitive food trucks (directly and indirectly) may start coming to college campuses, driving cover numbers down.

- License fees may go up to much higher levels.

- Food truck running and maintenance costs may be much higher than planned.

- Staff hired may not be as productive as previously thought or late or frequently absent.

- Seasonality and weather may play a much bigger role in the business than first thought.

- Finding the right/helpful parking spots is a constant challenge.

The purpose here, in both optimistic and pessimistic scenarios, is not to be complete in our analysis, or have one scenario win over the other, but merely to illustrate that startup founders need to wear both 'hats' and assess these possible outcomes early on as a risk-mitigating approach. This helps to better understand where these outcomes, both good and bad, can be addressed with new strategies or tactics (which is especially necessary in a fast-changing business landscape like this one).

As it happens, this case study shows a very positive business result, with Fresh-Fare making a good profit every year (including year 1) and even managing to pay Hector and Maria an increasingly strong wage for their efforts after year 2. In addition, both the balance sheet and cash-flows get increasingly healthier, meaning that the business may even be saleable as a going concern in the future if Hector and Maria choose to exit the business at some time.

Summary

This book, which describes the SLAM and GRAND diagrams in detail, is intended to be a helpful framework to guide ideators and entrepreneurs in a number of ways. These include helping them to:

- Identify the unmet need they are solving for and who, in customer target terms, has this issue more than others

- Assemble the best team possible to address the unmet need of this identified target customer

- Develop a product/service feature set or value proposition that is highly desirable to the identified target customers

- Confirm, through customer discovery, that founder guesses and hypotheses about what target customers want are accurate (by talking to a lot of them)

- Size the target market in terms of number of customers and in financial terms

- Evolve a go-to-market strategy that is likely to work in winning target customers to want to make a purchase

- Build a business model that is acceptable or even attractive to target customers to pay for the product and/or service being offered

- Research the existing market or sector the startup intends to enter and prepare to operate in the eco-system in the most successful way possible (and stand out from any competition)

In addition, this book seeks to help ideators and entrepreneurs who have validated their startup (by following the steps above) to build a highly robust execution plan that will help them focus and stay on track and grow steadily, and, in so doing, be attractive to any investors that the startup may need, especially when revenues and strong profitability will take time to build.

Finally, on the next four pages, are summaries of the SLAM and GRAND diagrams, including the three key questions that are critical to ask at each step.

Existing startup companies, as a collective set, drive any economy in the world much more than larger scale businesses, accounting for the majority of new jobs, innovation initiatives, and economic growth. We hope the GRAND SLAM methodology presented helps every startup have the best chance possible to join this group.

Summary of the SLAM diagram with 3 key questions at each step

④

Proof points that the channels, metrics and target customer segments are the right ones

⑤

Size of market calculations and speed of traction to breakeven given the investment (TAM, SAM, SOM)

M

①

Unmet need(s) and which segments (including the most likely 'beach-head') experience the most pains or gains that would be alleviated by your solution

⑧
Startup eco-system map
Competition and influencers and potential saboteur(s)

Buyers/end-users

②
Your startup and key team to tackle the unmet need

Suppliers/resources

P

③

Product or service offering and how it offers unique and specific value to each identified key segment with unmet need(s)

Direct and indirect influencers

⑦

Business model and monetization strategy and why (with support evidence)

⑥

Specific go-to-market channels that achieve greatest growth and traction (including gaining, sustaining and growing customers)

M = Market
P = Product/service

STEP 1 Unmet need(s)	1. What are the needs, pains, gains or what problems are you trying to solve? Why is now the ideal time to solve it?
	2. Does this problem matter at scale or is it local and/or relatively trivial?
	3. Who cares most about this problem/issue now or who is the target beach-head segment and buying persona (the actual 'average' person that you have in mind here)?
STEP 2 Key team	1. Which people are best able to get from 'Zero to 1' or focus on creating radical rather than incremental growth and why?
	2. Which people have the best capability and expertise to pursue this journey towards market-product fit for this target beach-head market?
	3. Which advisers can best steer the startup through the 'valley of death' and why?

STEP 3 Product or service offering	1. What MVP feature set best solves the problem(s) for the target beach-head market? 2. What is defensibly unique about the proposed/actual MVP feature set? 3. What is the best-prioritized product/service pipeline development strategy?
STEP 4 Proof points	1. What key assumptions of ours are we testing with customers (including what do we believe)? 2. What best questions do we ask of customers without 'leading the witness'? 3. How will we best assess the feedback we collect and best develop measures of future success?
STEP 5 TAM, SAM, SOM	1. How big is the total addressable market and is it big enough? 2. How big is the serviceable addressable market, and why? 3. How big is the serviceable obtainable market and why, and can we validate this top down and bottom up?
STEP 6 Go-to-market channels	1. Which major marketing channels best reach the target beach-head customers and why? 2. What is the priority order of the best marketing channels and how much money can/should we spend in each to maximize customer acquisition? 3. How will we best test each channel and change tactics based on our relative success and ensure have sound acquisition, retention and growth plans?
STEP 7 Business model	1. How much value do we create for customers and why? 2. What business or monetization model best fits the strategy for each target market(s)? 3. What is our cost of customer acquisition (COCA) and long-term value (LTV) created for our target beach-head customers?
STEP 8 Competition	1. How do we best design our startup to make a successful entry into the existing business eco-system and landscape? 2. How should we best evaluate and out-strip our perceived direct and indirect competition and saboteurs? 3. Who are our best/most optimal suppliers and influencers to maximize success and build defensible barriers to entry (create as near a monopoly as we can)?

Summary of the GRAND diagram with 3 key questions at each step

④ Capital raise and phasing

⑤ Capital deployment plans

⑧
Fiscal projections
P&L, 5 year revenue, COGs, expenses, profit and EBITDA

①
Detailed startup launch, growth path, and sustaining goals/timeline

②
Team resources and culture needed (internally and externally)

5 year cash flow including breakeven

5 year projected budget including fixed and variable

③
Pricing and assumptions (including COCA and LTV) to confirm long-term value and profitability

Major confirmed business assumptions (what we believe)

⑦ Infrastructure needs and make or buy decisions

⑥ Organizational systems design and support resources needed

STEP 1	
Detailed launch and growth path	1. In what way(s) do we launch or re-launch the startup with our newly established confidence that our journey towards product-market fit is on track?
	2. How do we best calculate our growth trajectory and the metrics/OKRs that will best track it with appropriate milestones to reach/aim for?
	3. What best growth and traction goals should we establish and then how do we best disseminate them to the team?

STEP 2	
Team resources	1. Which new people that should be progressively added directly to the team are best able to get from zero to 1 and help to reach our growth goals?
	2. Which external advisers, who should be progressively added directly to the team, are best able to help to reach our growth goals?
	3. What team and organizational culture and values should we craft and maintain to give the startup the best chance for long-term success?

STEP 3 Pricing and assumptions	1. What specific value do we add for our target customer(s) and how do we best demonstrate this? 2. How do we best price our product/service to convey great value and maximize our revenue and profitability goals? 3. How do we best calculate our cost of customer acquisition (COCA) at a granular level and determine the long-term value (LTV) of our target customer?
STEP 4 Capital raise and phasing	1. What capital do we need for the startup and at what point(s) will we need it, given our planned cash 'burn' rate and scaling plans? 2. What form should the capital raise take and can it be phased? 3. What sensitivity analysis should we have available to ensure that we can maximize our chances of using our invested capital wisely?
STEP 5 Capital deployment	1. In what specific areas will capital be spent and why? 2. In what specific and substantial ways will we be deploying capital (and how much of it) to acquire customers versus everything else? 3. How much estimated 'runway' will this capital give us, and when are we likely to need to raise capital again and how much (if we do)?
STEP 6 Systems design	1. What organizational design and management structure will serve us best over the short- to medium-term? 2. What are our best short-term HR processes (including hiring, compensation, EEO, diversity, etc.) going forward? 3. To what regulatory issues do we need to pay the most attention in the short- to medium-term and why (IP, Legal, Taxation, etc.)?
STEP 7 Make or buy decisions	1. What tasks or which processes do we absolutely want/need to keep in-house or do ourselves and why? 2. What tasks or which processes can we outsource/offshore or buy in to help keep our fixed infrastructure and overhead costs as low as possible? 3. What creative approaches can we take to getting startup work or tasks done and, in so doing, to conserve our cash?
STEP 8 Fiscal projections	1. On what key assumptions do our fiscal projections for the next three to five years rest and why? 2. In what areas should we have available sensitivity analysis on our fiscal projections and why? 3. What do our prospective P&L, balance sheet, cash-flow, and budget documents tell us about how we should best manage our business going forward?

Using the SLAM and GRAND diagrams for pitching

There are many good books and guides about building an effective startup business 'pitch-deck' and on how to present it well. However, it should not have gone unnoticed that the way that the SLAM and GRAND diagrams are built in single and progressive steps will ultimately help any startup CEO and management team to tell a story about the startup's journey from idea to becoming a company that, along with a reasonable amount of skill, helpful timing and good fortune, is going to grow and thrive in the marketplace in the future and will add value to its target customers.

On the SLAM side of the diagram, it is often best to follow the 8-step sequence in order, when preparing a presentation deck, and turn the startup's notes and answers to questions into summary slides.

For example, have slide 1 present what you deem the main problem or unmet need that you are solving for and who is your target customer. In the second slide, you can then present who is on the startup team and why they, with any advisers you hire, can solve the problem. In the third slide, you can present the overall product or service features and value proposition(s) that are likely to be most valuable to the startup's chosen customer targets.

Slides in a deck continue to be built in this way until a coherent story starts to emerge.

Although startups can use the GRAND side of the diagram to assemble further slides in a deck in the same way as on the SLAM side, it is less necessary to follow the sequence or even have all the data the startup gathers in all eight steps that are covered by the SLAM diagram.

In the main pitch-deck, investors are likely to want to see one slide on the amount of capital sought and on what it is going to be spent and another slide on the summary financials.

All the other data may be useful to summarize on slides but are typically only made available as appendices to the main pitch-deck to be used as called for.

All the other data may be useful to summarize on slides but are typically only made available as appendices to the main pitch-deck to be used as called for.

In the final analysis, there is never one way to build a pitch-deck so all of the above is offered as guidance only. However, investors will often expect to see this information either covered in the presentation (where sufficient time has been allowed of course) or discussed verbally at least. To do this well, startup founders are wise to prepare carefully and learn from every pitch that is delivered and make any necessary small adjustments each time.

Glossary of terms

'A' players. People hired by a startup who are demonstrably outstanding in either their skills or experience, as opposed to 'lesser' people – 'B' or 'C' players.

'A' round finance. Usually, a first institutional round of equity finance, coming from a venture or private equity fund or accredited investors.

Accelerator. Usually, a fixed-term, cohort-based program that includes seed investment, connections, mentorship, educational components, and typically culminates in a public pitch event or demo day.

Advisers. Expert or experienced people who advise or mentor or coach founders in a variety of ways including accounting, finance, sales and marketing, legal, HR, presenting, raising funds, and many other areas.

Advisory board. A group of startup advisers that usually work on retainer and/or have a small parcel of shares or share options in the business.

Angel investor. Typically an affluent individual (usually qualifying as a 'high net worth person') who provides capital for a business startup, usually in exchange for convertible debt or ownership equity.

ARR. Annualized Run Rate or often expressed as earnings last month then multiplied by 12 to get to ARR.

B2B. The startup is usually selling Business to Business.

B2C. Business to Consumer – the startup business is selling directly to the customer or consumer, sometimes called Direct to Consumer (DTC or D2C).

Balance sheet. A financial statement that lays out the company's assets, liabilities, and equity accounts till the date as reported.

Band-width. How much capacity a startup and its team of employees has to get work done with the resources (time and money) to do it.

Beach-head market. Focusing startup resources on one key area, usually a smaller market segment or product category, and winning that market first, even dominating that market, before moving into larger/different markets.

Black hat analysis. Author, Edward De Bono developed an analysis model called 6-hat thinking in which black-hat analysis is taking a very negative or pessimistic view in order to ensure all the possible harms to the startup have been identified.

Boiling the ocean. Pitching a startup as being capable of succeeding in multiple markets all at the same time or 'warming up' all the world's seas, all at once – possible but time-consuming and expensive.

Boot-strapping. The act of starting a business with little or no money, or on savings or credit, and investing what is progressively earned elsewhere.

Brand identity. A set of rules that define the look, sound, and feel of the startup, including brand logos, color, fonts, boilerplate copy, etc.

Break-even. When a startup has reached the point where it covers all expenses and generates a profit (and total sales or revenues equal its total expenses).

Build it and they will come. An approach in which the startup founder(s) build a product or service based on their assumptions and educated guesses and hope that customers will want what they have built – solution first, market need second.

Business eco-system. The existing business landscape in which the startup is likely to operate including competitors, suppliers, customers, influencers.

Business model. The rationale for or way that an organization creates, delivers, and captures value, in economic, social, cultural or other contexts.

Business Model Canvas. A one-page visual chart (created by Osterwalder and Pigneur) with nine boxes describing a startup's value proposition, infrastructure, customers, and finances.

Buyer or customer persona. Sometimes referred to simply as persona or avatar, this is the representation of a startup's ideal client or customer.

Cap table. A capitalization table is a table providing an analysis of a company's percentages of ownership, equity dilution, and value of equity in each round of investment by founders, investors, and other owners.

Capital. The money (drawn from loans, grants, equity or other sources) that is required to start a new business, whether for office space, permits, licenses, inventory, product development and manufacturing, marketing or any other expense.

Cash-burn. The rate at which a startup is losing money or spending more in reserves that it is in making revenues.

Cash-flow. A startup's operating cash-flow represents the cash actually available to meet the obligations of the business.

Churn (customer). Customer attrition, also known as customer churn, customer turnover, or customer defection, is the loss of clients or customers, expressed as a percentage.

COCA or CAC. The cost of customer acquisition or how much money needs to be spent to acquire a customer for the startup.

Co-creation. A process in which a startup and the possible solution provided works with target customers who will use the future solution to help design what it should and could look like and/or perform in functional terms.

Convertible note. A type of bond or debt that the holder can convert into a specified number of shares of common stock.

Crowd-funding. The practice of funding a project or venture by raising small amounts of money from a large number of people, typically via the internet.

Culture. The ways things are practically done in a startup organization or what people actually say and practice when the boss is not there to supervise.

Customer discovery. A process in which multiple target customers are interviewed one by one and usually face-to-face to test a startup's assumptions and hypotheses about the proposed business model.

Customer engagement. How much or often customers engage with a startup business. This often refers to how frequently they buy and/or how much they use a product or service (sometimes also called customer penetration and/or retention).

Customer research. Formal research on what customers want, often carried by survey or focus groups, and conducted to confirm product/service features are valuable and wanted (and usually done later than customer discovery).

Customer segment(s). Carefully identified and described segments or niches within an overall market that a startup might target.

Debt. A loan from a lender intuition or convertible note from other investors, which earns interest and should be paid back in a fixed timeframe.

De-risking a startup. The process of reducing the risk of startup failures, especially when third-party or outside investment is involved, usually by finding highly attractive customer segments, talking with people in the segment extensively and making sure they see the proposed product/service value and are willing to pay adequately (and at scale).

Early adopter. Sometimes also called pioneers, early adopters are the first to buy a product or service and will often give quick feedback on what they like and dislike.

Economic-buyer. The customer (person or person in business) who actually buys the product or service – and may or may not consume it.

Equity. The shares that a startup owns and allocates to founders, advisers, and investors.

Entrepreneur. A person who organizes and operates a business or businesses, taking on greater than normal financial risks in order to do so.

Excess capacity. Existing products or assets for which greater use/consumption can be created or wider deployment brought about (often by an intermediating platform).

Exit strategy. Startup founder's strategic plan to sell ownership to investors or another company—often used to reduce or liquidate a stake.

Feasibility. An analysis and evaluation of a proposed project to determine if it is technically and economically feasible, including profitable.

Feature set. A clearly prescribed set of product or service features or functionality, which tangibly adds value for the customer.

Fiscal projections. The financial forecasts or plans that a startup makes for the future, often over three or five years ahead.

Focus group. A group of likely target customers who are asked to focus on an early idea or proposal for a product or service and product input.

Follow on round. When additional capital (usually equity finance) is provided to top up a prior round, to help a startup to get to breakeven. Some startups need multiple rounds of capital over time or B, C, D and E rounds.

Founder(s). The original person or team that comes up with the startup idea and who bring the new company into existence.

Friction. The ways in which a customer experiences difficulty or frustration or inertia to cope when dealing with a current situation, product or service.

Go-to-market. A strategy for targeting given segments of the market and spending money in specific market channels to acquire customers and gain share.

GRAND. Goal, Results, Action, Navigational Device. Reverse side of the SLAM diagram.

Hustle. To implement tenacious and persistent follow-up while managing the precarious balance between being astute and being annoying. Hustling in business is not just a skill, it is an art.

Hypotheses. A theory about how a new product or service may better meet the needs of a set of target customers.

Ideator. A conceptual person who creates ideas for a possible new and potentially valuable product or service.

Inflection point. An event that results in a significant change in the progress of a startup and can be considered a turning point after which a dramatic change, with either positive or negative results, is expected to result.

Influencer. A person who has wide or far reach to a large audience of customers or businesses who may be attracted to buy a startup's product or service.

Intellectual property. A work or invention that is the result of creativity, such as a design, to which one has rights and for which one may apply for a patent, copyright, trademark, etc.

Iteration. The process of constant improvement after developing the initial version of something. In the startup world, it is usually very important to ship a minimum viable product so that you can start selling/raising money/etc.

Leading the witness. The process of asking the startup's target customer to comment on a product or service already conceived and/ or built without fully listening or being given time to provide their own unfettered input.

Lean startup. A methodology for developing businesses and products, which aims to shorten product development cycles and rapidly discover if a proposed business model is viable.

Life-style business. A business that aims to sustain a particular level of income and no more or to provide a foundation from which to enjoy a particular lifestyle.

LTV. The long-term value of a customer or how long a customer is likely to stay and buy again from a startup.

Make or buy decisions. Startups can often decide whether to do something themselves (make) or to get an outside company or partner to do it as a service (buy).

Market research. An organized effort to gather information about target markets or customers (often in demographic and psychographic terms) and discover details that are useful.

Market sizing. The effort to calculate the size of a given market – often by industry, geography, number of possible buying customers or some combination. Often conducted in TAM, SAM and SOM terms.

Marketing channel. The people, organizations, and activities necessary to transfer the ownership of goods from the point of production to the point of consumption. It is the way products get to the end-user, the consumer; and is also known as a distribution channel.

Metrics. Indicators of business performance that the startup identifies and uses to measure relative success of the operation at many levels.

Mindset. A mental attitude to life and business opportunity – Professor Carol Dweck at Stanford suggests that a growth mindset is needed over a fixed one.

Monetization. The way that a startup prices its product or services and thereby attracts sustainable revenue from its customers.

MVP. Minimum Viable Product or Proposition – typically a very early version of a product or service that has known faults.

NDA. Non-disclosure agreement to help to legally maintain confidentiality.

OKRs. Objectives, key results. A system for setting large-scale goals or objectives for the startup and then list what would represent a poor, average and good performance result.

Onboarding. The action or process of integrating a new employee into an organization and familiarizing him or her with the culture and with products/services.

Outsourcing. To obtain goods or services from an outside or foreign supplier (sometimes called off-shoring), especially in place of an internal source.

Overhead. The indirect costs or fixed expenses of operating a business (that is, the costs not directly related to the manufacture of a product or delivery of a service) that range from rent to administrative costs to marketing costs. Overhead refers to all non-labor expenses required to operate a startup.

P&L. Profit and loss financial statement for a business.

Pain and gain. The disadvantages, challenges, and frustrations for a customer in trying to get a task done (the pain) or the new freedoms in time or effort delivered if a new approach can be introduced (the gain).

Patent. A right granted to an inventor that permits an inventor to exclude others from making, selling or using the invention for a period of time.

Pitch/pitching. A presentation, typically supported by slides, in which a startup company's founder describes his or her company and seeks investment from angels or venture capitalists.

Pivot. A shift or change in business, product or service strategy to test a new approach regarding a startup's business model or product after receiving direct or indirect feedback.

Platform. Any hardware or software used to host an application or service.

Preferred stock. A form of stock which may have any combination of features not possessed by common stock including properties of both an equity and a debt instrument.

Product-market fit. The degree to which a product or service satisfies strong market demand. Product/market fit is the first step to building a successful venture in which the startup encounters early adopters, gathers feedback and gauges interest in its product or service.

Product/service roadmap. How a product is likely to extend or grow, to align the stakeholders, and to acquire a budget for it being developed – often applied to software development.

Prototype. An initial creation of a product that shows the basics of what a product will look like, what the product will do, and how the product operates.

Purchase order financing. A funding solution for businesses that lack the cash-flow to service customer orders. A financing company will often advance the startup money when it knows that it has a committed purchase order.

Razor/razor blade model. A business model wherein one item is sold at a low price in order to increase sales of a complementary good, such as consumable supplies. For example, inkjet printers require ink cartridges, and game consoles require accessories and software, or razors often need many blades.

Risk mitigation. A systematic process or methodology for identifying future startup risks and then coming up with ways to lessen or overcome them ahead of time.

Runway. The amount of capital that is left to deploy divided by the typical amount of monthly cash 'burn', usually expressed in months.

SaaS. Software as a Service or a method of software delivery and licensing in which software is accessed online via a subscription, rather than bought and installed on individual computers.

SAFE. Simple Agreement for Future Equity – a new form of funding for early-stage companies developed by Y Combinator to solve a number of issues with traditional convertible note funding.

Saboteurs. Competitors who are motivated to sabotage a startup, and its efforts to gain traction or market share, in a variety of ways.

Sales funnel. A model which illustrates the theoretical customer or buyer journey towards the purchase of a product or service – a four-step process could be 'awareness' (top of funnel), 'interest', 'decision' and 'action' (AIDA).

Seed round. Also known as seed funding or seed capital, this is a form of securities offering in which investors commit a small amount of capital in a startup company in exchange for an equity stake in the company.

Sensitivity analysis. The study and modeling of differently calculated outcomes (usually financial) or a set of numbers – used to model lower and/or higher pricing, customer numbers, market share, etc.

Side hustle. Any type of employment undertaken in addition to a full-time job. A side hustle is generally done as a freelance operator or for piecework or working, often for free, as a startup founder.

SLAM. Startup Launch Assistance Map – an eight step startup feasibility framework (with the GRAND execution diagram on the reverse side).

Sprint. A set period of time during which specific work has to be completed and made ready for review, usually in software development.

Startup. A company initiated by individual founders or entrepreneurs to search for a repeatable and scalable business model.

Supply chain. The identification of all individual points of supply between the startup and its suppliers to the ultimate consumer.

TAM, SAM, SOM. Measures of market size. Total Addressable Market, Serviceable Addressable Market, and Serviceable Obtainable Market.

Traction. A measurable set of customers or users that serves to prove to potential investors that a startup is acquiring customers steadily (and on a rising basis) and therefore 'going places'.

Trademark. A recognizable symbol, word, or words legally registered or established by use as representing a company or product.

Unit economics. The fundamental minimum piece of a startup business that can be measured to understand where revenue comes from. It's whatever best represents the exchange of value which drives the business. For example, a unit for a SaaS startup might be a customer; for a car dealership, the unit may simply be a car. For all startups, it includes COCA and LTV.

Unmet needs. The potential for customers to get a better outcome or experience significant improvement over their current approach or practices.

USP. Unique Selling Proposition. Describes the benefit a startup offers, how it solves customers' problems and distinguishes it from competitors.

Validation. A rigorous appraisal of whether startup founders original hypotheses are born out and can lead to a successful business being created.

Valley of death. The period between a startup's initial funding and the end of its runway. If you get through here, you should be OK.

Value adding. The process of determining how a startup explicitly adds value to a customer in tangible and intangible ways, often as a precursor to determining a fair price to charge.

Value proposition. How a startup's product solves customers' problems or improves their situation (relevancy), delivers specific benefits (quantified value), tells the ideal customer why they should buy from the startup and not from the competition (unique differentiation).

Values. These are typically abstract ideas that guide organizational thinking and actions, including beliefs in broad aspirational items such as service, teamwork, quality and more personal ones such as humility or fun.

Variance analysis. The difference between a budgeted, planned, or standard cost and the actual amount incurred/sold. Variances can be calculated each month or quarter for both costs and revenues.

Velocity. A measurement of how fast a startup is making money or quickly leads are moving through the pipeline and how much value new customers provide over a given period.

Vision. A startup founder's view of what the future could and should look like when they have eventually brought his or her product or service to market. In the world of entrepreneurship this often runs counter to current practice or belief by most people.

'We believe' statements. Assumptions and hypotheses that startup founders believe at the earliest stages that have yet to be tested with real customers without leading them in any way.

What-if thinking. Thinking which imagines a completely different way to solve for a customer's unmet needs. This often comes by asking questions such as, 'What if this were reversed?', 'What if this were analogous to something else?' or 'What if we eliminated an entire step?', etc.

Working capital. The accessible cash or operating liquidity available to a startup.

Y combinator. A US-based seed accelerator, started in March 2005. Y Combinator is consistently ranked at the top of US accelerators, graduating well-known companies such as AirBnB, Reddit, Stripe, DropBox, Doordash, etc.

Zero to 1. The process of creating something radically new and taking it to the first step (or intensive growth). The phrase is used in contrast to the term '1 to n' (or extensive growth), which means creating incremental improvements to what is already familiar.

Acknowledgments

No book, even when it is as short as this one, is written by one person alone and I am grateful to many people who both made input suggestions over many months and read earlier versions of the final product you now see.

First and foremost I'd like to thank my partner and wonderfully supportive wife and the best coach I have ever encountered, Anne Sandberg, my friend and book publisher of 25 years, Kerry Milin in Australia and my friends and colleagues Professor Jim Spee, who wrote the foreword to this book, and Paul Notaras for his expert input on all the case study financials in this book. I am also very grateful for the many entrepreneurial conversations with my youngest son Nathan Warner via Skype in Australia.

Others worthy of special mention are David Bell, Alex Bitoun, Jason Booth, Scott Collins, Chip Conley, Michael Dorman, Barry James Folsom, Mimi Grant, Fred Haney, Ulya Khan, Huinan Liu, Joanna Medin, Arlen Meyers, Larry Morgan, Harry Nelson, David Norris, Rosibel Ochoa, Blake Petty, Justin Radeka, Rigo Saborio, Art Salyer, Steve Sharp, Matt Stodder, Mark Tepper, Jeff Tidwell, Ted Whetstone, and Ellen Young who all made extremely valuable contributions to my thinking, whether they know it or not (I am not always the easiest person to whom to make suggestions).

Finally, I'd like to acknowledge entrepreneurs the world over. These few brave, and some would say 'foolhardy', individuals take big steps into the unknown that most of us simply will not take. In so doing, they sometimes help the world to solve problems that seemed insurmountable. I hope this small contribution to how current and future entrepreneurs may 'de-risk' their efforts as they take these big leaps is useful to them.

Jon Warner
California, August 2019

Notes

Notes

Notes

Notes

Notes

CPSIA information can be obtained
at www.ICGtesting.com
Printed in the USA
LVHW040723260819
628924LV00023B/710/P